LINGUISTIC PLANETS OF BELIEF

Linguistic Planets of Belief presents a way for people to notice, examine, and question the role language plays in identifying, recognizing, and understanding those around them. This book introduces the metaphor of 'planets of belief' as a framework for understanding both the connections of language and identity, and the reasons we hold these perceptions so dear. It explains why we make up our minds about who people are and what they are like, even if they have only spoken a few words to us, as well as how language can dictate what we think of others as a whole. In doing so, it:

- Takes a large survey of linguistic research in the field of perceptual dialectology and assesses hundreds of accounts of people and their speech from hundreds of respondents.
- Uses maps at the state, regional, and national level in the US to expose how our linguistic perceptions of geographical regions cluster into planets of belief.
- Challenges readers to critically assess these assumptions and empowers readers to shift the way they think about language and to understand why they stereotype others based on speech.

Equipped with such a large data set, *Linguistic Planets of Belief* explains the patterns that labels from perceptual maps show us and will make you consciously aware of the interaction between language use, perceptions, and stereotypes. It is essential interdisciplinary reading for students of English language, linguistics, and sociolinguistics, and will also be of interest to anyone concerned with the ways that language, ideology, and discrimination intersect.

Paulina Bounds is Associate Professor of Linguistics at Tennessee Tech University. Her research focuses on perceptions of speech in the United States, especially in the American South. She uses methods of perceptual dialectology to investigate differences and similarities in national- and state-level perceptions. She has presented her work at numerous national and international conferences and has published papers in the *Southern Journal of Linguistics* and the *Journal of Linguistics Geography*.

Jennifer Cramer is Associate Professor and Chair of the Department of Linguistics at the University of Kentucky. Her research focuses on the perception and production of linguistic variation at dialect and regional borders, with a specific interest in the dialects spoken in Kentucky. She co-edited *Cityscapes and Perceptual Dialectology* (with Chris Montgomery, 2016), and she is the author of *Contested Southernness: The Linguistic Production and Perception of Identities in the Borderlands* (2016).

Susan Tamasi is Professor of Pedagogy and Director of the Linguistics Program at Emory University. Her work focuses on attitudes toward linguistic variation, Southern identities, and social and political issues connected to American English dialects. She is the co-author of *Language and Linguistic Diversity in the US: An Introduction* (with Lamont Antieau, 2015).

LINGUISTIC PLANETS OF BELIEF

Mapping Language Attitudes in the American South

Paulina Bounds, Jennifer Cramer, and Susan Tamasi

 Routledge
Taylor & Francis Group

LONDON AND NEW YORK

First published 2021
by Routledge
2 Park Square, Milton Park, Abingdon, Oxon OX14 4RN

and by Routledge
52 Vanderbilt Avenue, New York, NY 10017

Routledge is an imprint of the Taylor & Francis Group, an informa business

© 2021 Paulina Bounds, Jennifer Cramer and Susan Tamasi

British Library Cataloguing-in-Publication Data
A catalogue record for this book is available from the British Library

Library of Congress Cataloging-in-Publication Data
A catalog record for this book has been requested

ISBN: 978-1-138-49112-0 (hbk)
ISBN: 978-1-138-49113-7 (pbk)
ISBN: 978-1-351-03382-4 (ebk)

Typeset in Bembo
by Deanta Global Publishing Services, Chennai, India

In loving memory of Carol Preston, who supported us all with love and grace.

CONTENTS

FIGURES

TABLES

PREFACE

Have you ever noticed how quickly you can make up your mind about who people are and what they are like, even though they have only spoken a few words to you? How is it that language can dictate what we think of others? This book, as a whole, presents a way for people to notice, examine, and question the role language plays in identifying, recognizing, and understanding those around them. A wide range of research has shown that we need very little linguistic evidence to make judgments about people (e.g. Purnell, Idsardi, & Baugh 1999; Lambert 1967). While there are many subtle (or not so subtle) cues that allow people to make decisions about who a person is, such as how they are dressed, what music they listen to, or what they do for a living, few of these are as telling as someone's speech. Even the tiniest bit of language – whether someone says *you*, *y'all*, *yinz*, or *youse*, for example – can lead to a fully developed conclusion of who that person is and whether or in what way you want to interact with them. In other words, language is a trigger that activates strong, complex beliefs about who the speaker is, and we only need a word or two to make up our minds about them.

To set the stage for the book, the first two chapters set the theoretical framework for understanding the data and our analyses that follow in Chapters 3 through 5, with Chapter 6 concluding our exploration of linguistic perceptions. Therefore, Chapter 1 defines and describes the concepts of perception, belief, and stereotype to contextualize the ideas described above. Specifically, we need to understand these concepts to know how it is that one word might trigger various kinds of ideas about the person speaking. We also situate the role of language and stereotypes in a range of interdisciplinary research on the topic and introduce the idea of planets of belief with ample discussion of how a visualization of the planets can lead to a better understanding of ideas about language, culture, and people. Chapter 2 introduces perceptual dialectology as a research paradigm that allows for the systematic analysis of nonlinguists' beliefs about language and linguistic variation. We showcase the subfield, including its data collection, data processing, and analytical procedures, and highlight how the production of labels by nonlinguists has been essentially overlooked within the research conducted in this approach. In the next three chapters we focus on the data itself.

As an example of the application of the linguistic planets of belief metaphor, we spend Chapter 3 exploring the ideas our respondents have about the speakers and their language varieties in the US. Drawing on our own national- and regional-level data, as well as data from other perceptual dialectology studies, we describe the planets of belief that the data reveal. Chapter 4 zooms into specific beliefs about one linguistic corner of the world – the American South. For many Americans, the American South is a culture so embroiled in misinformation and mythologies that its true nature is not easily understood. Therefore, we thoroughly showcase the stereotypes held about Southerners, not only in terms of their language but more broadly as well. In the final data chapter, Chapter 5, we zoom even further in into particular states to showcase how granular our planets of belief can be. For one, the labels employed on maps of Tennessee, Kentucky, and Georgia reveal that the way the respondents see their state differs from how they see their region or even their whole country. Although all three states are included in the perceptions of the South in the many national- and regional-level perceptions, when we zoom into state level, the respondents differentiate between areas that they consider Southern and those they do not. The results indicate that our regional experiences and beliefs may have contrasting and contradicting impact on our language ideologies. In the final chapter, we reexamine the concept of linguistic planets of belief as it applies to the kinds of linguistic beliefs revealed in our data. We explore the overall patterns as well as the general lack of patterns found in some parts of the analysis to highlight the role of identity in language attitudes and the perceptions of language varieties.

This book showcases the good and the bad; the structured and the chaotic; and the nuanced complexity that underlies the quotidian nature of language and our attitudes toward it. It is our hope that, in the end, readers will find that their belief planets can benefit from close examination. While disruptions to belief systems are often difficult, we espouse the beliefs that knowledge is power and that this book provides knowledge that many readers may have never encountered.

References

Purnell, Thomas; William Idsardi; and John Baugh. 1999. Perceptual and phonetic experiments and American English dialect identification. *Journal of Language and Social Psychology* 18.10–30.

Lambert, W. 1967. A social psychology of bilingualism. *Journal of Social Issues* 23.91–109.

ACKNOWLEDGMENTS

This book took a lot of work and support from a great number of people to be fully carried out. First, we would like to thank all of the anonymous respondents who tirelessly circled and wrote on maps and gave us their ideas and opinions about language around them. Moreover, we would like to thank Emory University's Center for Faculty Development and Excellence and the Emory College of Arts and Sciences for providing financial support for editing, indexing, and permissions. A huge thank you to our wonderful copyeditor, Lamont Antieau for his countless suggestions and probing questions that shaped our three voices into one. We would also like to thank Hanna Enlow and Cecilia Carroll for combing through numerous data sets and previous presentations, and Chuck Sutherland for producing maps for Chapters 3 and 5. We are truly appreciative of Dennis Preston and the many colleagues who gave us feedback on early presentations of this material. Additionally, we are very thankful for our editorial team at Routledge, particularly Adam Woods who patiently supported us through the writing and submission process.

Paulina would like to thank her husband Halsey, and kids – Marielle and Freddie – for daily support, push, and reinforcement, but also plenty of joyful distraction, laughter, and late-night conversations about the book and everything but. Many thanks are also needed to her parents, sister, and friends for continuing enthusiasm about the book and mental support throughout this process. She would also like to thank Wes Cecil for inspiration that influenced and shaped a lot of ideas presented in this book, and Cody Matthews for always unfinished discussions about language, which turned into pages of ideas – a seed for this book. And finally, thank you to Jennifer and Susan for all the amazing conversations that made this book happen, but also made our friendship one for a lifetime.

Jennifer would like to thank her husband Aaron for making sure she stayed somewhat balanced while trying to teach, research, chair, parent, and breathe during this whole process. She also wants to thank her children – Isabelle, Nathan, Benjamin, and Georgia – for making her turn off the laptop sometimes to play games, watch movies, and be silly. Finally, Jennifer gives thanks also to the student researchers at the University of Kentucky, especially those involved in the collection of the Kentucky state maps, for helping bring these perceptions to light.

Susan would like to thank her students and colleagues for patiently listening while she figured out how to articulate 20 years' worth of thoughts about language attitudes in the South. She would also like to thank Jamie Martin for his continued help with images and for no longer asking, 'Is that book done yet?'

1

CONCEPTS OF BELIEF

Perceptions, beliefs, and stereotypes

Every single day of our lives, in every second of our daily routines, we are bombarded by visual, auditory, and other stimuli in the world around us. The movement of the leaves on a tree catches your eye, a strong breeze messes up your 'good hair day', or perhaps the smell of blooming jasmine brings back a memory of your grandma's kitchen table. How we organize, identify, understand, and interpret these stimuli is called PERCEPTION. It is what allows us to take lower-level information (like the smell of jasmine) and convert it to higher-level information (like grandma's house), which in turn might be further connected to good or bad feelings (e.g. loving grandma).

The APA defines perception as

> the process or result of becoming aware of objects, relationships, and events by means of the senses, which includes such activities as recognizing, observing, and discriminating. These activities enable organisms to organize and interpret the stimuli received into meaningful knowledge and to act in a coordinated manner.
>
> (Bargh & Chartrand 2000)

Our entire lives consist of a conglomeration of perceptions. But perceptions are not merely received; they are shaped by our experiences and, in turn, shape what we think about the world around us. In the example above, we perhaps knew nothing of jasmine until we first experienced those beautiful, flowered branches at grandma's table. In fact, we might have never even really known they were from a plant that is commonly called 'jasmine'. But our exposure to a specific smell, combined with our grandma experiences, and those experiences being generally pleasant, means that each time we encounter that smell we are reminded of those fond times, even those that did not occur at the kitchen table.

Such an example makes it obvious that perceptions are quite important in our day-to-day lives. What is perhaps less obvious is the full nature of perception. We know that perception is not merely a receptive system; it is also reactive, and it is influenced by a person's previous experiences, ability to learn, quality of memory, etc. (e.g. Kahneman 2011). While perception relies on complex functions in the nervous system, it appears to be quite effortless, as we tend to be unaware of these processes. Additionally, even given only minute stimuli, patterns in our perceptions are created, and our reactions to those stimuli can become predictable, robust, and even difficult to modify. Returning to the grandma example above, if the situation were such that in every instance in which you were in your grandma's house involved smelling jasmine and dusting her curio cabinet, you might make a larger connection to jasmine that involves things like grandma, love, cookies, porcelain dolls, sneezing, old people, old houses, and more. If such connections are made, it's possible that the right sensory input will bring up any one (and perhaps all) of these other thoughts. Further, it might also cause you to make certain generalizations, like 'old people have dusty houses' or 'grandma has to keep jasmine around to cover up the old house smells'.

These patterns are handy, easy, and effective for us to rely on; we do not need to re-evaluate our circumstances from scratch each time. Their power resides in the fact that they can be both below the level of consciousness and automatically activated (e.g. implicit bias, as in Babel 2016). These kinds of overgeneralizations are sometimes referred to as STEREOTYPES. Social psychologists minimally define stereotypes as 'qualities associated with particular groups of people'; however, recent research has expanded this definition: 'Stereotypes not only reflect beliefs about the traits characterizing typical group members but also contain information about other qualities, such as expected social roles and characteristics of the group' (Dovidio & Jones 2019:276–77). These patterns have to do with groups and individuals and how society is necessarily composed of both. As McGarty and colleagues (2002:1) state, 'Without individuals, there could be no society, but unless individuals also perceive themselves to belong to groups, that is to share characteristics, circumstances, values and beliefs with other people, then society would be without structure or order'. These kinds of structures can be helpful to us, cutting down on processing power and allowing people to interact in ways that suggest some kind of shared knowledge.

However, they can also be harmful. For example, if you decide, hypothetically, that you would like to go to your favorite local donut shop, but you find several police cars there when you arrive, you will likely pass it by, whether consciously or unconsciously, because you have arrived at the conclusion that either (1) there is trouble (i.e. the police are there in their capacity as police officers, perhaps to arrest someone), in which you don't want to be involved, or (2) the store has likely run out of the good donuts because the police officers have eaten them all. While the first response is perhaps simply a statistical one, the second one draws heavily on a media-propagated stereotype that police officers eat a lot of donuts (with the additional meaning that they spend more time eating donuts than doing their jobs). Whether police officers actually eat more donuts than the average person is irrelevant; the choice of foregoing a visit to a donut shop because of a stereotype in this instance means that this belief has a real impact on the day-to-day lives of the people who hold it. People use this 'knowledge' to drive their decisions.

While we might consciously know that stereotypes are not true, we also hear people say things like 'Stereotypes don't come from nothing'. Although it may seem contradictory, both sides are right. On the one hand, we know that stereotypes are not true for each and every individual because they cannot be truthfully applied to the group as a whole. With regard to the donut example above, we know that not all police officers eat a lot of donuts. On the other hand, this type of default police officer, who is not a real person but a combination of perceptions cobbled together, is commonly used as a model to be applied to real people (e.g. Babel 2016). Our experiences with police officers, whether direct or indirect, can lead us to an assumption that officers eat too many donuts, so that even if we happen to see police officers at a fruit market, we may believe that they must have just come from the donut shop (and therefore haven't been doing their job). When we activate stereotypes, we lose nuance and detail – as we can't get beyond the stereotype.

Stereotypes and perceptions are both tied up with BELIEFS, often so much so that the terms are used interchangeably by some. The term ATTITUDE also sometimes joins a list of similar terms (e.g. Fishbein & Raven 1962). Belief can be conceived of as 'the intersubjective mechanism linking cultural scripts, frames, codes, and ideologies with their inferred effects on observable lines of action' (Strand & Lizardo 2015:45). Within a framework of belief like that of Bourdieu (e.g. 1977, 1990), we can conceive of beliefs as part of one's HABITUS, or a set of ingrained, deep-seated habits, dispositions, and practices that contribute to the ways in which people experience their social worlds. Habitus is acquired through imitation within socialization processes in a society and is therefore shared widely within the community. Because of its widespread nature, habitus serves to shape how individuals in a society act, and thereby creates its environment.

Studying belief and perception is complex. The structural nature of belief within the sociological tradition suggests that people hold on to their beliefs even when confronted with contradictory facts because of the deep-seated nature of these structures (Babel 2016). Still, we know people have the ability to change. In this book, we want to recognize the nature of connections between belief, perception, identity, and language, and present an explanation of why people hold linguistic perceptions so dear. To do so, we introduce the metaphor of PLANETS OF BELIEF (Carroll 2016). First, however, we must understand the interdisciplinary research that has previously been conducted on perception, belief, and language.

Interdisciplinary views on perception and belief

Perceptions allow us to make connections between experiences. Beliefs provide a structural framework for understanding these experiences and connections. As complicated, multifaceted concepts, perception and belief have held a place in the social sciences for decades. While an exhaustive review of these concepts is beyond the scope of this book, here we present a brief overview of different areas and key findings that have been found in social psychology, language attitudes research, philosophy, and linguistics. Throughout this book, we hope to show that our work on the perceptions and beliefs attached to linguistic variation, viewed through the planets of belief metaphor, complements and extends previous work on the subject (rather than contradicting it or attempting to replace it).

Social psychology

There are many different paths one can choose to follow when looking at concepts of belief and perception in the field of social psychology. The vast body of robust research on the subject includes approaches ranging from schema theory to category activation, from confirmation bias to attitude polarization, and from naïve realism to language attitudes (see below). As indicated above, we know that people use previous 'knowledge' as a means to reduce the process of recognizing, identifying, and reacting to others. Once a sensory stimulus activates particular ideas about an object or experience, then other beliefs that have been previously connected are also activated: the smell of jasmine leads to a childhood memory, which leads to a positive emotion or to missing grandma. Mental concepts are connected to one another, in categories or schemas, and the thought of one can access a part or the whole of a category. According to Aarts and Dijksterhuis (2002), 'Research in social cognition and social judgment shows that our perceptions of other people are affected by knowledge activated previously', and in 'forming an evaluation of a person, people use categories that are mentally accessible' (123).

Additionally, once a belief is set, it is set fast and is very difficult to change. Even when presented with information that questions or even directly contradicts one's views, a person will cling to the schema that they recognize and believe in. Ross and Ward (1995) present naïve realism as a means for not letting go of beliefs. They contend that our social understanding relies on convictions, one of them being that 'the failure of a given individual or group to share my views [because] the individual or group in question may be biased' (Ross & Ward 1995:111). These views are further solidified through confirmation bias, in which people interpret new information in ways that confirm the beliefs they already hold and readily dismiss ideas that do not fit into their pre-formed categories or that contradict the reality of such categories. People embrace that which supports their beliefs and dismiss that which contradicts their pre-formed views.

In their book *The Enigma of Reason* (2019), Mercier and Sperber present the concept of MYSIDE BIAS, noting that while people are good at finding problems with other people's arguments, they overlook similar problems inherent in their own beliefs. This highlights the individuality of perceptions and beliefs, despite the fact we share experiences and pass ideas to one another. While we might share overlapping categories or schemas that contain and shape perceptions, each person's view is unique and individual.

Social psychologists are generally concerned with the investigation of attitudes toward group membership, characteristics that influence interpersonal relationships, and the link between an individual's behavior and group membership. They are also interested in the development and distribution of attitudes within a society. A profitable approach to this line of research has been in the investigation of language use as a reflection of these attitudes. In this, '[a]ttitudes toward particular varieties are … taken to be attitudes toward speakers of those varieties' (Ryan et al. 1982:2).

Language attitudes

Traditional language attitude research began with the work of Wallace Lambert in the 1960s. Lambert had become interested in investigating the social attitudes of French and English speakers in Quebec when he overheard two English speakers on a bus talking about the two French speakers seated behind them. Lambert retold what he witnessed:

> My attention was suddenly drawn to the conversation in front wherein one lady said something like: 'If I couldn't speak English I certainly wouldn't shout about it', referring to the French conversation going on behind them. Her friend replied: 'Oh, well, you can't expect much else from them'. Then one of the ladies mentioned that she was bothered when French people laughed among themselves in her presence because she felt they might be making fun of her. This was followed by a nasty interchange of pejorative stereotypes about French Canadians, the whole discussion prompted, it seemed, by what struck me as a humorous conversation of the two attractive, middle class French Canadian women seated behind them. The English ladies couldn't understand the French conversation, nor did they look back to see what the people they seemed to know so much about even looked like.
>
> (1967:92–93)

After overhearing this conversation, as well as other comments about language differences, Lambert focused on the creation of a 'systematic analysis of the effects of language and dialect changes on impression formation and social interaction' (1967:93).

For this investigation, Lambert and others (1960) created an interesting and reliable research method in the form of a matched-guise test. As part of this test, a group of informants (or judges) are asked to listen to recordings of speakers of two different languages who are reading translations of the same passage. The judges are then asked to evaluate the personality characteristics of each speaker, using only linguistic cues. While the judges believe they are listening to and evaluating different speakers, they are actually hearing the same speaker in different guises. Therefore, as each speaker controls for rate of speech and other suprasegmental features, character judgments are based solely on the language variety that is being used rather than the speaker.

In conjunction with the matched-guise test, speaker evaluations are often assessed through the use of semantic differential scales. For example, Lambert (1967) specifically asked his judges to evaluate speakers in terms of 18 different personality traits. These traits were grouped into three distinct categories: competence (e.g. intelligent, ambitious, self-confident); personal integrity (e.g. dependable, kind, sincere); and social attractiveness (e.g. sociable, affectionate, likeable). This combination of matched-guise tests and semantic differential scales has been found to be very effective in revealing judges' 'private reactions', especially when compared to the results of direct questionnaires (Lambert 1967).

In his studies of language attitudes toward Quebecois speakers of English and Canadian French, Lambert (1967) found significant patterns. The evaluations were biased against the French speakers and showed more positive attitudes toward the English speakers. For example, the English speakers (or rather, English guises) were judged to be better looking, more intelligent, kinder, more dependable, and even taller than their French counterparts. What is most interesting about this finding is that the same attitudes existed regardless of whether the judges were speakers of English or French.

This line of research quickly developed into a large body of work, and further research was conducted on language attitudes in bilingual communities. For example, Lambert, Tucker, and d'Anglejan (1973) continued work on French and English; Wölck (1973) researched Spanish and Quechua; Ryan and Carranza (1975) looked at Spanish and English; and Lambert broadened his own scope of research and studied Hebrew and Arabic (Lambert, Anisfeld, & Yeni-Komshian 1965). Furthermore, language attitude research extended beyond bilingual studies to include perceptions of non-native accents (Anisfeld, Bogo, & Lambert 1962; Sampson & Palmer 1973; Ryan 1973), second language acquisition (MacNamara 1973; Gardner & Clement 1990), language and gender (Sachs, Lieberman, & Erickson 1973; Kramarae 1982), and African American English (Tucker & Lambert 1967; Fraser 1993).

Aligning with the goals of social psychology, language attitude research has found that judges do view speech as an indicator of group membership. And more specifically, speaker evaluations tend to follow a status versus solidarity division. Judges who themselves speak a nonstandard variety generally rate standard speakers high in terms of status issues, such as intelligence and ambition, but evaluate other nonstandard speakers as being more loyal and honest. Edwards (1982) says that evaluations of language varieties [...] do not reflect either linguistic or aesthetic quality per se, but rather are expressions of social convention and preference which, in turn, reflects an awareness of the status and prestige accorded to the speakers of those varieties.

(21)

This finding is quite important, as it has been used to further investigate the influence of individuals' attitudes toward group membership on their social behavior. Applications of this research include Roberts, Davies, and Jupp's (1992) work in language and discrimination, as well as the investigation of teacher perceptions of students by Altman and Taylor (1973) and Carranza (1982), and student perceptions of teaching assistants (Rubin & Smith 1990, Rubin 1992).

In the early 1980s, this line of research again broadened its scope, as investigators examined the development and distribution of language attitudes. Rosenthal (1974) found that children between three and five can make judgments on dialect differences and often show a preference for their home variety (in Day 1982:119). Furthermore, Day (1982) found that language attitudes are a part of a person's communicative competence and are, therefore, acquired. While children first present positive attitudes toward their home language, by the age of ten they have already developed the attitudes of the dominant culture and attribute greater prestige to the standard dialect. They also recognize negative attitudes associated with their home variety during this stage (Day 1982; Giles et al. 1983). Additionally, St. Clair (1982) examined the actual distribution of all social attitudes (including language attitudes) throughout society and provided examples, such as social Darwinism and the eugenics movement, of the social ideals of standardization and normalization being promoted. He posited:

If the mainstream of society has been socialized through the educational system and through the mass media to accept a certain belief system, they will attempt to please and impress one another in their speech behaviour and in the contents of their attitudes. It is this reinforcing pattern of behaviour that accounts for the category of well-behaved citizens.

(St. Clair 1982:173)

Philosophical approaches

Our concern with reality and what we define as 'real' has been a quest of philosophers for centuries. However, we are left to decide whether to judge our world on how well it corresponds with the truths that we hold (Aristotelian model) or to see our world as being coherent within this framework of our mental system. Or we can try to combine the two, in order to have a world that makes sense to us (coherence model) and corresponds to the truths we hold (correspondence model) (Cecil 2019). What complicates these matters even further is that, following Nietzsche, 'we have no grounds for *knowing* whether our most basic beliefs correspond to the way the world is, however necessary it is for us to continue to rely upon them for our survival' (Nehamas 1985:46). This ignorance is something with which we all struggle in life, but at the same time, we do not question it, choosing instead to operate under the assumption that we are right about the world around us. Such confidence allows us to survive; we could not possibly accomplish even the most basic tasks if we had to question and reconsider each and every one of our beliefs on a daily basis. Therefore, we have to commit to some ideas, adopt a perspective, and use that perspective as a lens through which to see the world around us. As Nehamas (1985:49) pointed out, that perspective cannot encompass all the views, but instead we have to decide on a specific outlook:

> We must assign a greater relative importance to some things than we do to others, and still others we must completely ignore. We do not, and cannot, begin (or end) with 'all the data'. This is an incoherent desire and an impossible goal. 'To grasp everything' would be to do away with all perspective relations, it would mean to grasp nothing, to misapprehend the nature of knowledge. If we are ever to begin a practice or an inquiry we must, and must want to, leave unasked indefinitely many questions about the world.

We can understand this to mean that people must choose what data they take in and use in their daily lives, and ignore the rest. We may convince ourselves that we are being objective, but that is not exactly what is happening. Instead, most of the time we will follow our beliefs, patterns, and habits to decide what to do with any new data. Oftentimes, we do not choose consciously to think in these ways, but rather, these processes are encultured and engrained in us by how we are raised and by the cultures within which we live.

Across linguistics

Of course, the language that we use to describe the world also impacts our perceptions of it. Sapir (e.g. 1921) emphasized that

> it is quite an illusion to imagine that one adjusts to reality essentially without the use of language and that language is merely an incidental means of solving specific problems of communication or reflection. The fact of the matter is that the 'real world' is to a large extent unconsciously built up on the language habits of the group. We see and hear and otherwise experience very largely as we do because the language habits of our community predispose certain choices of interpretation.
>
> (Whorf 1941:36)

This statement makes a very strong assertion that our world is our language, and our language is our world. Indeed, this is the thinking behind the theory of

LINGUISTIC RELATIVITY often referred to as the SAPIR-WHORF HYPOTHESIS, which essentially says people build their worlds in their minds because of the language that they use. The more deterministic version of this hypothesis that was the focus of Sapir's approach is generally less accepted in the field of linguistics and has been controversial (e.g. language determines thinking). A much less rigid version that suggests that language CAN influence thinking and culture (and vice versa) is more widely accepted today (Wolff & Holmes 2010).

Either way, under such assumptions, our beliefs are an integral part of the process. Consider how differently we may approach what our goal in life is if we describe it in two different but seemingly similar ways: 'I want happiness' versus 'I want joy'. Although on the surface these utterances may seem very similar, the two differing words have different connotations. *Happiness* often relates to external factors that can make us happy, like seeing puppies or eating ice cream (Cecil 2019). On the other hand, *joy* is more of an internal, sensual feeling that we have more control over (ibid). We can feel joy because we are not relying on external factors to make us happy. We can choose to have joy in our life, but we don't have much control over happiness (ibid). In this way, using just two different words that are similar in some aspects may put us on two different life paths.

The magnitude of the influence of language on our thought process and our reactions to the world are perhaps best understood within the context of Whorf's THOUGHT WORLD: 'the microcosm that each man carries about within himself, by which he measures and understands what he can of the macrocosm' (Whorf 1941:47). According to such a view, our inner world is extremely important for our interactions in and with our external reality. It is unclear if we can and do distinguish between the two, as Whorf explains in the following example:

> When we think of a certain actual rosebush, we do not suppose that our thought goes to the actual bush, and engages with it, like a searching light turned upon it. What then do we suppose our consciousness is dealing with as we are thinking of that rosebush? Probably we think it is dealing with a 'mental image' which is not the rosebush but a mental surrogate of it. But why should it be natural to think that our thought deals with a surrogate and not with the real rosebush? Quite possibly because we are dimly aware that we carry about with us a whole imaginary space, full of mental surrogates. To us, mental surrogates are old familiar fare. Along with the images of imaginary space, which we perhaps secretly know to be only imaginary, we tuck the thought-of actually existing rosebush, which might be quite another story, perhaps just because we have that very convenient 'place' for it.
>
> (1941:49–50)

As portrayed by this example, our minds have a vast imaginary space to hold the world we experience. It also holds this world as it changes in time and space and what we believe about it. Our ideas and thoughts about rosebushes and other entities are shaped by language, and this is the basis of how we act. 'People act about situations in ways which are like the ways they talk about them' (Whorf 1941:48). If we think about the happiness/joy example above, we can see how the language that is used shapes what we do. If I frame my goal in life as happiness, my path will be different than if my goal is joy, and I will look at the world differently. In this way, thoughts and the language with which they are produced have a great deal of power and influence over what we do.

This power of language also appears in its relation to how we think about the world around us. As Lucy (2005:301) says,

> Whorf questioned the existence of a single ideal relation of language to reality and in precisely this sense he also questioned our conceptualization of a unitary reality, since its qualities would vary as a function of the language used to describe it.

The questioning of the single ideal relation of language to reality leads to uncertainty about reality itself. We can't trust language to describe reality, so we can't trust reality itself. Thus, any universals that could be applied to language are impossible to prove, and if we cannot prove them, then no language can be judged as superior or inferior, because without universals, we lack a language-neutral standard against which to judge anything in language or reality (Lucy 2005). If we don't have standards (and these are understood here as standards of judging the relationship between language and reality), we don't know how to value the world around us. We take the incomplete information that we get from language describing reality and use mechanisms such as GESTALT, the idea that we can fill in incomplete ideas to make them whole, or activate stereotypes to fill in the gaps. Based on incomplete information, we can still create values because we must still deal with the reality around us.

Lucy (2005) continues to explain the potential trap created by the relation between language and reality:

> Only by acceptance of the conventions of one or more particular languages can we speak at all and so gain the advantages of having language support for sophisticated cultural and psychological activities. But this same acceptance of a particular language commits us to the specific conventions of that language and to their consequences for our thinking.
>
> (307)

In this view, we are stuck. Our language creates affordances and boundaries of our experiences with reality, and to a large degree, we have no choice in that. For one, we don't get to choose the language community we are born into. Additionally, most of us don't ever question the conventions our language commits us to because, to truly notice that, we would have to be exposed in a substantial and systematic way to self-analysis (e.g. by becoming a linguist or other language expert) or to a different language and culture.

For example, extensive research on cross-linguistic differences, work that examines how we perceive reality in different languages, seems to suggest that various linguistic structures influence how we construct reality. In varied and extensive research conducted on this matter (e.g. Fausey & Boroditsky 2011; Flusberg & Boroditsky 2011; and Thibodeau & Boroditsky 2011), we find example after example of how languages perform differently in various cultures. In a study conducted on Spanish and English (Fausey & Boroditsky 2011), speakers were asked to describe agency in a case of an accidental breaking of an object and an intentional breaking of an object. Results of this study suggest that English structurally requires agency in the sentence structure more than Spanish. English speakers in the study pointed to the agency of 'culprits' more than Spanish speakers (Fausey & Boroditsky 2011). Therefore, the researchers point to the way that English codes agency as the reason that we remember it more.

Such a structural dependency can influence us tremendously, as described in an example below:

> For example, English speakers who read a report about Justin Timberlake and Janet Jackson's wardrobe malfunction containing the agentive expression 'tore the bodice' not only blamed Timberlake more, but also levied 53% more fines than those who read the non-agentive 'the bodice tore'. Further, this linguistic framing had a big effect on blame and punishment even when people watched a video of the event and were able to witness the tearing with their own eyes.
>
> (Fausey & Boroditsky 2011:151)

This shows that a pattern in which an event is described can overwrite what is actually observed and can be established strongly, typically through repetition. 'The way events are typically talked about in a linguistic community and what people encode and remember about these events even when they are not talking' (Fausey & Boroditsky 2011:156). Therefore, if we encode things a certain way, and this encoding becomes what we remember about events, people, and our reality, this information is fed back into our belief system, and the beliefs are further solidified. As such, our belief system is not dictated by our senses alone; it is structured by the rules of the language we use and how we use it. Stunningly, this particular power of language goes unnoticed in our everyday lives.

Another linguistic power that we generally don't pay attention to is the metaphors we use in language and how much they influence our way of thinking about the world. For example, Schon's (1993) work on GENERATIVE METAPHOR shows that the language one uses to discuss a topic sets not only how one understands the concept but also how it is applied, such as in the creation of social policy. Similarly, in a study conducted twice over a period of a few years (first in 2011 and again in 2015), we can see that metaphors play a key role in how we perceive the world, such as if a crime is described as a *virus* or a *beast* (Thibodeau & Boroditsky 2011, 2015):

> In five experiments we investigated the role of metaphor in guiding how people reason about the complex problem of crime. We found that metaphors exert an influence over people's reasoning by instantiating frame-consistent knowledge structures, and inviting structurally-consistent inferences. Further, when asked to seek out more information to inform their decision, we found that people chose information that was likely to confirm and elaborate the bias suggested by the metaphor – an effect that persisted even when people were presented with a full set of possible scenarios.
>
> (Thibodeau & Boroditsky 2011:9)

The experiments showed that the metaphors chosen to frame an event have a tremendous influence on how we think about the event. Subjects were more likely to propose preventative measures when using the virus metaphor and to offer more punishment-oriented solutions when using the beast metaphor. Furthermore, it seems that one doesn't even have to remember the metaphor that was encountered to be influenced by it. When subjects were asked to highlight the most important information in the descriptions of the crime situation, none of them pointed to the metaphor (Thibodeau & Boroditsky 2011:9).

Metaphors seem to organize the way we see the world and understand it. As Lakoff and Johnson claimed 40 years ago, metaphors are what we live by:

> Our concepts structure what we perceive, how we get around in the world, and how we relate to other people. Our conceptual system thus plays a central role in defining our everyday realities. If we are right in suggesting that our conceptual system is largely metaphorical, then the way we think, what we experience, and what we do every day is very much a matter of metaphor.
>
> (1980:3)

In this view, metaphors are what we do. Any type of input we receive from our senses that needs to be illustrated in words happens through this lens of metaphor. Lakoff and Johnson further describe the pervasive nature of metaphor as an inherent substance of our culture, stating,

> Cultural assumptions, values, and attitudes are not a conceptual overlay which we may or may not place upon experience as we choose. It would be more correct to say that all experience is cultural through and through, that we experience our 'world' in such a way that our culture is already present in the very experience itself.
>
> (1980:57)

Therefore, the role and function of a metaphor seem to be essential to our functioning in the world. If metaphors are inherently intertwined in our culture, we cannot simply isolate them and choose to use them or not. They are part of us, and we encounter them quite early in our enculturation process. Because of this, we never question or examine them. But most importantly, the power of metaphors reveals itself in how much it dictates our lives:

> Metaphors may create realities for us, especially social realities. A metaphor may thus be a guide for future action. Such actions will, of course, fit the metaphor. This will, in turn, reinforce the power of the metaphor to make experience coherent. In this sense metaphors can be self-fulfilling prophecies.
>
> (Lakoff & Johnson 1980:156)

As the examples above show, the concepts that we use in language create and shape the reality in which we live. The reality we create is one in which we act. We do not act in isolation, but we act under the influence of our culture's metaphors and beliefs. Most of the time, we are not aware of the impact of these cultural products, and we do not feel the need to question these beliefs because they are accepted by the members of our communities.

Sociolinguistic modeling of perception

Moving to sociolinguistics, the field within which our own work is situated, an important focus related to perception has been on what are called LANGUAGE IDEOLOGIES, or 'sets of beliefs about language articulated by users as a rationalization or justification of perceived language structure and use' (Silverstein 1979:193). These ideologies are 'the cultural system of ideas about social and linguistic relationships, together with their loading of moral and political interests' (Irvine 1989:255). They are specific to the context within which they are enacted and are constructed over time (Kroskrity 2004). Their creation depends on both direct input, such as experiences with specific speakers, and indirect input (Edwards 1999), such as media-propagated stereotypes about speakers. For example, someone may have specific beliefs about people who speak with New England accents, and those beliefs may come from a combination of their experiences with actual people from the region and from depictions of people purportedly from the region broadcast via radio, television, film, and the Internet. Such ideologies are not permanent; they are dynamic and intricately connected to not only the linguistic form that is produced, but also to who produces it, as well as when, where, and to what effect it is produced (e.g. Woolard 1992).

Research focusing on language ideologies has revealed that the primary motivators for many beliefs about language are situated on a status vs. solidarity continuum and are closely tied to notions of belonging (e.g. Preston 1989; Hartley 1999). For example, Luhman (1990), in examining how students at a university in eastern Kentucky felt about Appalachian dialects in comparison to standard dialects of American English, revealed that acceptance of a low-status stereotype of Appalachian English was less likely among students who identified with Appalachian speech than those who did not. These same students were also more likely to believe that Appalachian speech was used by wealthy, successful people. On the other hand, the students who did not identify with the standard speech samples still assigned higher status to those varieties than the Appalachian ones, even though solidarity measures were consistently higher for Appalachian voices. See Chapter 2 for a longer discussion about these kinds of studies.

Interestingly, individuals are rarely consciously aware of the reasons behind their gut reactions to various linguistic productions (e.g. Uleman & Bargh 1989). For example, if you were to ask someone why they cringe when they hear someone pronounce *pen* as if it were *pin*, they would likely just respond that it sounds like nails on a chalkboard or that it 'sounds dumb'. For others, however, this pronunciation would go unnoticed because that's the pronunciation typically heard in their larger speech community. Once cognizant of the 'nails on a chalkboard' interpretation, the latter individuals might temper their own reactions (and even their productions, if possible). The power of language ideologies is embedded in their ability to make language users self-conscious about their own speech.

When we endeavor to study these subconscious reactions, we are engaged in a study of LANGUAGE REGARD (e.g. Preston 2010). These ideologies impact the construction of one's linguistic self and of the linguistic other we might be describing. Indeed, language regard centers on how the thoughts, beliefs, attitudes, and actions of nonlinguists can help us best understand language and variation (Preston 2010). In such explorations, it is clear that

> [f]ocusing on the evaluation of linguistic forms by speakers themselves allows for clearer insight into the cognitive processes that motivate linguistic choices, and the study of language regard permits an analysis of the attitudes and ideologies that come to bear on identity constructions and encourages analysts to delve deeper into this confluence of macro- and micro- level phenomena.
>
> (Cramer, Tamasi, & Bounds 2018:62)

Within this paradigm of language regard (and even in other areas of sociolinguistics), the question must become one of how to model the cognitive organization of these ideologies, beliefs, and attitudes about language (e.g. Babel 2016).

This type of exploration engages with how any concept can be represented in the mind, which necessarily means dealing with how thought is constructed. One such model involves using exemplar theory, or the idea that individuals take a new stimulus and categorize it based on its similarity to the exemplars they already have stored in their memory, to model how linguistic experiences are connected. Drager and Kirtley (2016) constructed an exemplar cloud to depict how we use numerous automatic processes (in addition to exemplars) to process linguistic and social information in our day-to-day lives. The easy availability of such cognitive processes, combined with our innate desire to categorize entities immediately, results in quick judgments, even when there is little input. For example, research has shown that Americans are fairly good at identifying the race of an individual (when the choices are Anglo, Black, and Hispanic) upon hearing only one word – *hello* (Purnell, Idsardi, & Baugh 1999). Thus, using an exemplar model of language ideologies, we can understand the reasons that underlie our reactions to language and can begin to see why variation such as that described above in the *pen* example might occur.

However, an appeal to cognition alone cannot answer all of our questions about processing language ideologies. We know that individuals process both linguistic and non-linguistic information in arriving at their language perceptions. Countless matched-guise studies (e.g. Lambert 1960; Lambert 1967; and others discussed above) have shown that social information has at least as much impact if not more on how we hear language. Campbell-Kibler's (2016) work modeled the formation of language attitudes from this perspective, highlighting how a spectrum of social factors becomes interconnected with linguistic factors, revealing the extent to which these types of information are intrinsically linked.

The connection of the social and the linguistic is most evident when an individual encounters a mismatch. Rubin (1992), for example, showed that, in rating international teaching assistants, university students rated Asian instructors poorly, even when the voice heard in the matched-guise test was using a standard English variety, indicating that the presumed facts can override the 'real' facts, as illustrated by the Timberlake/Jackson example above. Indeed, there is a phenomenon called ACCENT HALLUCINATION (e.g. Rubin & Smith 1990; Rubin 1992; Fought 2006) that has been found to occur when someone's appearance suggests the presence of one accent even though a different one is encountered. McGowan's (2015) understanding of speech perception, however, indicates that such failings and hallucinations might be best described by the concept of CONGRUENCE. In his modified matched-guise experiment, when listeners encountered the incongruent condition (Caucasian face + Asian-sounding accent), their ability to understand what was said was diminished when compared to the congruent condition (Asian face + same Asian-sounding voice). This suggests that the cognitive model must account for more than linguistic and social information as separate entities, but rather as interrelated components of the same system.

One final model that might be useful in understanding language ideologies is Preston's ATTITUDINAL COGNITORIUM (e.g. Preston 2010, 2016, 2018). An example of this model can be seen in Figure 1.1. The system, which draws on Bassili and Brown (2005), makes this interconnectedness of linguistic fact and social impact explicit. It showcases how beliefs and structures form together as a neural network. Individual components of this network 'are complexly interconnected, some with well-traveled and/or direct pathways, allowing stronger and quicker associations; others are more weakly or indirectly connected' (Preston 2010:12).

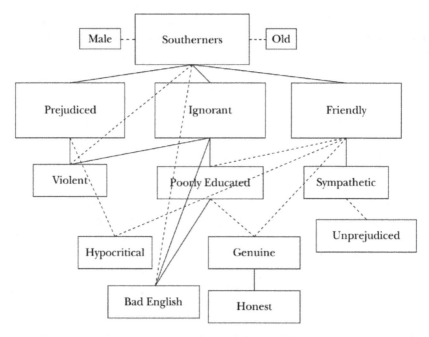

FIGURE 1.1 Attitudinal cognitorium of Southernness. Source: Courtesy of Preston (2018).

The example presented here focuses on notions of SOUTHERNNESS in the United States, which will be elaborated on in later chapters.

Even though these theories about and views of beliefs and perceptions are presented through separate disciplines, this does not mean that they necessarily work against each other. In fact, as we recognize the key points of each, we realize that they can and do complement each other, and in some ways this bolsters the findings. They all generally agree that there are connections between how people see and experience the world, linguistic and otherwise, and that they draw on these pieces of information to understand and process the world within which they live. In concert with these approaches, this book presents another potential model for understanding these connections. We draw on the preceding discussions about the importance of perception, how thoughts, beliefs, and attitudes are constructed and enacted, and the role of language in creating our vision of the world, to produce a model that also engages with our understandings of how the universe works. Our visualization of how language ideologies operate and are organized is based on Sean Carroll's (2016) planets of belief metaphor, which is described in detail below.

Planets of belief

To get a sense of how language ideologies are intertwined with the experiences of real language users in their language-using contexts, we introduce the metaphor of planets of belief as a framework for understanding both the connections of language and identity and the reasons we cling to these perceptions. Sean Carroll, a cosmologist and theoretical physics professor at the California Institute of Technology, uses the metaphor of planets of belief to explain how we make sense of the world in his book *The Big Picture: On the Origins of Life, Meaning, and the Universe Itself* (2016). In it, Carroll presents the metaphor in this way:

> Planets don't sit on foundations; they hold themselves together in a self-reinforcing pattern. The same is true for beliefs: they aren't (try as we may) founded on unimpeachable principles that can't be questioned. Rather, whole systems of belief fit together with one another, in more or less comfortable ways, pulled in by a mutual epistemological force.
>
> (2016:108)

In elaborating on the seemingly unchangeable nature of beliefs, Carroll adds, 'We're faced with the problem that the beliefs we choose to adopt are shaped as much, if not more, by the beliefs we already have than by correspondence with external reality' (2016:121). Indeed, it is this notion of a disconnect between belief and reality that makes the metaphor seem so well suited to the description of language ideologies. As we'll see in later chapters, the things people say about language varieties (and people, places, etc.) sometimes bear little resemblance to the things research shows about these language varieties (and people, places, etc.).

We also know that we create ideas about life (and language) through interacting with people around us, but we rarely, if ever, meet a person who shares all of our beliefs. Thus, our beliefs are not stable, concrete, and static, but rather, they work more like the planets described by Carroll, who says that

> [a]bandoning the quest for a secure foundation in favor of a planet of belief is like moving from firm ground to a boat on choppy seas or a spinning teacup ride. It can make you dizzy, if not seasick. We are spinning through space, nothing to hold on to.
>
> (2016:110)

The reason we are able to make snap decisions about people is because we have systems of belief that we create and carry throughout our lives. These systems are made up out of our daily experiences, observations, and perceptions, and like the formation of a planet, gravitate together piece by piece, particle by particle, to build a whole system. We make assumptions about people based on their speech, dress, behavior, ethnicity, etc., and all of these ideas are pulled together with gravitational forces. When we encounter a person, then, all we need is to recognize one particle from our planet of belief to trigger and activate everything that we know that this planet has. With time, we become more and more protective of our planets; it is hard to change our minds about things we believe in.

Our planets of belief are created mostly unconsciously, but what makes them powerful is that, even without knowing it, they dictate how we act in our daily lives. We use them to make judgments about others, with speech as one of the most common triggers. But if our planets are built out of faulty and harmful particles, they make us repeat and maintain negative stereotypes about people, and we act accordingly. Their strong defense mechanisms prevent us from seeing people any differently, no matter how many contradicting pieces of evidence we encounter. That healthy, fruit-eating police officer mentioned earlier is still believed to be a closet donut lover. And as such thoughts are really a product of our subconscious mind, we often don't ponder about them explicitly in a regular manner.

One way that the metaphor of planets of belief can serve as an organizational visualization of our perceptions is in relation to the concept of awareness of language variation. As Squires (2016:81) explains, '[A]wareness seems to be a matter of the raising of internal knowledge to the surface of a speaker's consciousness, with a continuum of awareness representing a continuum from knowledge that is implicit to explicit'. Planets of belief can be seen as the network of connections that is mostly implicit and unconscious in speakers' minds. At times, this internal knowledge rises to the surface when speakers are confronted about their beliefs, or when they are asked about them explicitly, for example, in the form of the draw-a-map task that is common in PERCEPTUAL DIALECTOLOGY, an area of research that deals with how nonlinguists view their dialect landscapes (see Chapter 2). While we recognize that facts won't always change someone's mind (e.g. Kolbert 2017), the planets of belief metaphor suggests that it would take some kind of explicit impact to create a possibility for change. To confront the perceptions and stereotypes that we hold in our planets, we need to face them.

In addition, Squires distinguishes between perceiving and noticing in relation to awareness. 'Things are frequently perceived without being noticed' (Squires 2016:82). With regard to the creation of the planets of belief, such a distinction is crucial because the particles that create our planets are delivered by our senses in a mostly unconscious manner, without us noticing them. We probably only make so many conscious choices about our beliefs because of this. But we do seem to transfer the unconscious patterns to our conscience mind. We are capable of articulating our beliefs about the world. If we are able to do that, the question remains: Do we really choose these beliefs (e.g. Whorf 1941)? How much does the input we have around us influence what our beliefs end up being? Do we really get to decide what we believe about something, or do we only decide to change the beliefs once we have them (cf. Lucy 1997, 2005)? Although no explicit answers can be found in the planets of belief metaphor, it is important to uncover the relationship between the unconscious and conscious parts of our mind. The network relations of the particles reside mostly in our subconscious mind, unnoticed by the part of us that we call ME. We act upon the dictates of our stored and organized perceptions, and we don't even notice. Therefore, the difference between perceiving and noticing is crucial in considering the planets of belief, because only when we take notice of our own planets can we have any chance of changing stereotypes and negative judging into something more positive, more productive.

Our perceptions feed our actions, as evidenced by the results of a series of experiments on perception and noticing in subject–verb agreement variation. Squires (2016:101) explains: If participants perceived the non-standard sentences as forms that English speakers might plausibly produce – as sociolinguistic variants rather than errors – that was not evident in their self-reports. It is a non-trivial task for future work to understand the cognitive processing that moves one from the perception of linguistic forms to their interpretation as socially meaningful. This observation provides further evidence that if we could understand the structure and process of how our perceptions behave in our minds, we would be able to explain speakers' behaviors better. We believe that the metaphor of planets of belief provides a visualization and proposed organization that allows experts to frame their ideas about language better, while also offering a way to speak to non-experts about how and why we may think of others in the ways we do.

What we're asking in this book is this: What if we could expose these planets of belief? By examining their formation, can we understand the beauty that exists within planets full of positive perceptions? Can being explicit about our language ideologies act as a meteor that destroys those planets full of negative stereotypes? Within this book, we look at research that has been done in linguistics, specifically perceptual dialectology, to expose planets of belief. The results of research performed in this tradition, where everyday speakers tell researchers explicitly what varieties of language they perceive and what they think about people who speak in various ways, allow us to bring the pieces of these planets into the light. We have collected, categorized, and described hundreds of accounts of people and their speech from hundreds of respondents using various data types. Equipped with so much data, we can explain the patterns that appear, and using the metaphor of planets of belief, we can present a picture of the complex cognitive processes that are at work.

Visualizing the metaphor

The exploration of perceptions and our cognition of them shows that perceptions are crucial in understating our linguistic and social behaviors. The ways that others have modeled perceptions, especially Preston's (e.g. 2018) attitudinal cognitorium, provide support for our own understanding of how the interconnectedness of language and perception might be organized. We believe that the metaphor of planets of belief provides a way to visualize the structure of language attitudes and presents a proposed form of organization that allows language attitude researchers a better way to frame their ideas about language, offering a way to speak to non-experts about how and why we may think of others and their language in the ways we do. If we can imagine how our planets of belief work, we can better understand them, and be more aware of how we can change them. We believe that the metaphor allows us to pull various models together and provides a common way to talk about them.

The key to understanding the visualization we propose is to better understand the application of the metaphor to language attitudes, using the notion of planets of belief as a heuristic for the classification of various linguistic attitudes, beliefs, and perceptions. As indicated above, the fact that planets are suspended in space and remain in orbit through self-supporting mechanisms, and not because they are securely situated upon foundations, can be applied to linguistic perceptions by thinking of the impenetrable nature of such perceptions. They do not exist as fact, yet they continuously perpetuate themselves across an individual's life through their experiences. We also know that planets are not themselves composed of solid components, but are instead simply made of particles held together by gravity (Carroll 2016). If this is also true of beliefs, the question then becomes 'What holds these belief worlds together?' And just as the ground that we walk on creates the illusion of a sturdy surface to step on without having to think about the imperceptible forces that allow the Earth to move in space, stay on the orbit's track, and remain intact, so too do perceptions operate. We need not think of them with each encounter; they are automatic, self-reinforcing, and impactful in ways that essentially control us beyond our own awareness.

If we consider that our beliefs could be organized this way, we can begin to explore how various experiences, impressions, and ideas about the world stick together. We can see how our notions about language can be part of a larger system, or, more precisely, as a piece of the belief planet encompassing everything we think about the world. Such a model allows us to understand that our perceptions of language and everything else in our lives are inherently intermingled, not floating in isolation. Instead, they are pulled together in a unified, systematic way to form a planet that is unique to us. We have visualized this concept as Figure 1.2 (Cramer, Tamasi, & Bounds 2018:449), which 'is a potential visualization of a belief planet, where each individual dot stands for one belief'. To take a non-linguistic example, we can envision a belief planet about food. If one of the dots in Figure 1.2 represents an individual's belief that pizza is tasty, the nearby dots might provide additional pertinent information on which types of pizza are worth eating (e.g. some people prefer thin crust; others prefer deep dish) and those that must be avoided (e.g. one should/should not put pineapple on a pizza). Other dots might be what we could call 'pizza-adjacent': perhaps they have to do with when it is good or bad to eat pizza (e.g. is pizza an appropriate breakfast choice?), ideas about places where we usually get pizza, and which places have good pizza AND pasta. The list could go on, but the point is clear. A person's food belief planet includes information about pizza and other foods, but also the other things related to food, such as where we eat it, who we like to eat it with, the person who introduced us to a particular dish, the members of the culture from which a certain food originated, and maybe even what you think of their culture beyond the food, potentially including the language spoken by people from that

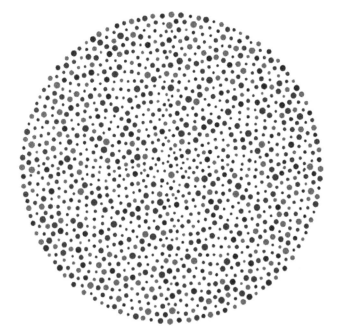

FIGURE 1.2   A hypothetical belief planet. Source: Courtesy of Cramer, Tamasi, & Bounds (2018:449).

culture. In the image, some dots are bigger than others; we estimate that some beliefs are more dominant than others in our belief planets, and as such, we have represented some beliefs as larger components of the visualization.

When we visualize our belief system as planets, it is easy to see them as sturdy, impenetrable rocks. However true this view can be from afar, when we zoom in on the planet, as in Figure 1.3, these particles are connected, and the links represent the beliefs that are so closely interconnected as to activate one another easily. The idea of the planets allows us to suggest that beliefs are related in this way and are likely grouped together within the planet. It makes sense that some ideas will group together more easily, but an important point of the interconnectedness is that all interactions are possible. As we have said elsewhere, 'All beliefs have the ability to interact with one another, and as such, the ability to reinforce or even change one another' (Cramer, Tamasi, & Bounds 2018:450). The zoomed-in belief planet in Figure 1.3 relates to being a resident of the US South. The ideas show an interconnectedness of where people are born or live with notions of wide-ranging beliefs about intellect, education, trustworthiness, and other ideas. These ideas are potentially triggered together (e.g. Preston 2010) or separately. We believe this visualization to be similar in nature to Eckert's (2008) indexical field, in a specific way highlighting 'the interconnectedness of beliefs, the overlap of categorization of beliefs, as well as the notion that some beliefs are not so easily categorized' (Cramer, Tamasi, & Bounds 2018:450).

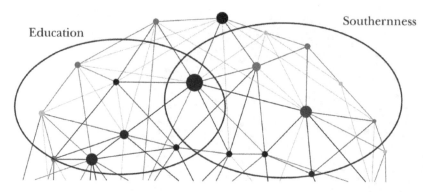

FIGURE 1.3 A zoomed-in hypothetical belief planet. Source: Courtesy of Cramer, Tamasi, & Bounds (2018:450).

As indicated above, the visualization suggests that beliefs are not only interconnected but also likely to be activated together. The interconnectedness is perhaps like a fractal (e.g. Mandelbrot 1982), grouped together and recursive, intricately composed of the many kinds of beliefs that are inherent to the numerous and varied parts of our lives (e.g. food, religion, education, language, etc.). The connections are endless, and having the ability to impact one another and activate others is quite like how particles are described in quantum physics: 'particles can be organized in fractals, and our ideas, experiences, and perceptions can interact with each other in an infinite loop of patterns' (Cramer, Tamasi, & Bounds 2018:450).

If we consider the depiction in Figure 1.3, we can think of the activation of the various components of Southernness and education (see Chapter 4) when someone hears something like *fixing to*, a phrase commonly used in the US South (or by people elsewhere with connections to Southernness or perhaps African Americanness). The hearer's mind will access not only the word's denotation (if they know it) but also the many potential connotations of it, including attitudes and perceptions of the speaker and, in this case, a particular set of beliefs surrounding the concept of SOUTHERN. Through the various combinations of our perceptions and the language that we use to project them, as speakers and hearers, we create various iterations of reality through our minds. But because of shared cultural schemas (see below), actual personal experiences, and the like, there is a strong possibility that the hearer, upon understanding the phrase that has been uttered, will make specific connections outside of those specifically connected to Southernness, which, in our example, have to do with education. Perhaps they believe that someone who would say this phrase has had little education. Perhaps they know that use of linguistic variants has nothing to do with education. Either way, especially in the American context, language and education have been intimately linked (e.g. Macaulay 1977), and hearers are likely to make these kinds of connections, even if they are actively unaware of doing so. This reality is not created through a conscious, well-thought-out process; it is automatic and instantaneous (e.g. Kahneman 2011). Thus, we conceive of these potential combinations as being interconnected like planetary particles held together by a gravitational force, a process that happens without the help of the particles themselves.

Returning to the food planet above, perhaps quite obviously, this example need not be completely separate from linguistic attitudes. Maybe someone holds the belief that someone who uses the word *hoagie* to refer to a long sandwich instead of *sub* is ignorant. Or maybe individuals hate people who use the word *coke* to refer generically to carbonated beverages. Ultimately, we think it's unlikely that our beliefs about any one thing could be detached completely from our beliefs about other things. There is a natural interconnectedness of beliefs about all things we encounter (and even things we don't, like unicorns) because of the high level of similarities of experience across human cultures. We would argue that this can be seen through the lens of a CULTURAL SCHEMA, or 'the story you tell yourself about things (and people and events, etc.)' (Burkette 2016:92). Schemas provide a structure and an organization for understanding the world in which a person lives. Kretzschmar (2009) uses schema theory to account for such similarities, calling them 'an array of characteristics out of which a pattern is generated' (224), with a focus on the fact that these mental representations are held broadly within a community but operate at both the individual and cultural levels. Recently, this approach has generally become more widely accepted than PROTOTYPE THEORY (e.g. Kretzschmar 2009), in which category membership is determined on the basis of similarities to some prototypical item.

In time, beliefs can become like a hard piece of rock in our planet. Although a piece of rock feels hard to the touch, we know that particles are in constant movement, so we can think of the relationship between matter and energy in terms of our beliefs being energized by daily input from the world. As the mass expands, it becomes more difficult to free the energy that is trapped inside of it. Similarly, as our beliefs expand from the input we receive through our senses, it becomes more difficult to free the energy trapped inside of them to change them and reconfigure the mass. In this way, the more consolidated our beliefs are, the more easily we absorb the inputs around us into these beliefs, thus making it harder to change the formation of these belief planets. The energy that is trapped in this metaphor is the positive or negative valuing of a belief, so that when we think of 'releasing' this energy, we think about how difficult it is to destruct the mass and change our minds about beliefs we hold.

Our planets are held together by a gravitational pull of compatibility and exclusiveness. When we think about the importance of first impressions, we know that what we experience first has the power to become a strong particle in the planet, and confirmation of such experiences will attract ideas that are similar to them to create a network of particles (see Kahneman 2011 for a discussion of different mental systems). For example, if your first encounter with a new food, pickled herring, for instance, is a positive one, the next time you are presented with anything pickled or anything herring-related, it is likely that you will be open to it and may even enjoy it. If you didn't enjoy it the first time, then the completely opposite scenario can unfold, potentially to the point of discouraging you from trying any new foods. Taking it one step further, someone who already has a tendency toward conservatism with respect to food (e.g. a picky eater) may not even need the initial bad experience to believe the food will not be enjoyed, thus further solidifying the tendency.

It seems that a robust, coherent planet is composed of all of our thoughts, experiences, and associations, and it holds together every conviction provided by our unconscious mind. Our silent, subconscious mind constantly provides new input to be compared against our already existing beliefs and against the world that we constantly encounter to quickly react to what we perceive around us (e.g. Kahneman 2011). Such constant work allows for us to have a coherent planet that is continuously confirmed to adhere to the world that we call 'real'. It is a comfortable place to be; it makes us believe that we already know what this concept/person/entity is all about, that we are correct in our perceptions of them, and that our expectations have been set appropriately (Cramer, Tamasi, & Bounds 2018).

Planets of belief against the world

Our perceptions, when conceived of as being shaped into planets and organized into fractal connections of ideas and impressions of others, are what we use to interact with others. If we meet a new person, we don't need to get to know them extensively to decide what we think of them. We use our planets for that. We hear a word, a phrase, an idea, or a particular pronunciation, and it can activate a whole collection of interconnected perceptions and ideas that we can attribute to the person with whom we are interacting. This is similar to PRIMING, or the idea that exposure to one stimulus might influence a response to a second stimulus even without intention (e.g. Bargh & Chartrand 2000), in the context of the organization of mental lexicon. In such processes, our brain activates all possibilities of a word immediately upon hearing the first sounds of it (Curzan & Adams 2006), essentially the same as the process of typing a word into a Google search box and having all of the various possibilities appear. It may seem like a great deal of extra work for our brains to do, and we may think that waiting for what the speaker will actually say is more efficient, but Curzan and Adams (2006) explain that the usefulness of priming is that it

> could actually be a mechanism for speeding language processing. Because priming activates words that are likely to appear in the immediate context of the word you have just read or heard, you will be able to process the entire utterance more quickly as you are 'prepared' for what is likely to follow.

(218)

In this way, both priming and our notion of planets of belief make activation a key component. The main difference, perhaps, between lexical priming and the triggering of fractal networks in a belief planet is that, during priming, the collocations and connotations that didn't adhere to the actual utterance get discarded when a phrase activates a group of ideas about the speaker. But those ideas do not necessarily get eliminated, which is how the planets metaphor can aid in our understanding. Even when a belief has been shown to be false, the belief remains.

We have been talking about planets of belief as a combination of the various impressions we gather from the world around us and the processes in our minds that we use to organize those impressions in ways that allow our minds to process the world more efficiently and effectively. Those impressions are made out of the stimuli that our senses encounter within the world. Anything that we see, hear, touch, sense, and think can contribute to the body of experiences that we rely on. Language is crucial in that the conglomeration of impressions that we gather and react to can be our only way to access our sentiments, including our understanding of speakers and how they experience the world. Language is a powerful trigger for our ideas about the world and people. As will become clear in Chapter 2, asking people to draw and write on maps, as is common in the field of perceptual dialectology (e.g. Preston 1989), or to talk about other people and their speech, is a way that we can understand the interconnected nature of perceptions and language. In this way, we can begin to uncover and describe the structure of our planets and the parts of them that we share with others.

Are the triggered impressions and memories a true representation of the person that we are interacting with? Is this a shortcut that can cut short our openness to figuring out all the complexities of the people around us? It seems there is a potential threat in relying on our unquestioned beliefs and perceptions in these matters. People cling to such beliefs and perceptions, feeling that they can comfortably ignore other possibilities and deciding that they have enough information to make up their minds about an individual based solely on these initial activations of their belief planet. While these impressions might be accurate, maybe even true, others will be off the mark. And even if they are true, they may be negative or harmful. Of course, there is likely little problem in assuming that a person is honest and nice. But the danger of misjudging and treating others wrongly according to other perceptions is fairly high. What makes these negative perceptions even more dangerous, if not examined, is that when they are activated unconsciously, they may dictate more than just what and how we think. They may cause us to act in discriminatory ways, choosing not to hire someone or offer them available housing (e.g. Purnell, Idsardi, & Baugh 1999) simply because of how we react to their language. A planet of belief is not positive or negative in and of itself, but we must question how it is used in both positive and negative ways. It is a useful processing mechanism, but its usefulness is only apparent when we examine it and become aware of how our planets work so that we can become PURPOSEFUL users of it.

As described above, the planets of belief metaphor is a powerful tool for our minds to use as we try to understand the world around us. On the one hand, it allows us to extrapolate what is going on in our minds in a metacognitive way. We can name and describe trends and patterns that we see in perceptual data. On the other hand, it can enable those introduced to the metaphor to begin a journey of seeing what their own planets are like, in order to better understand their own specific reactions to various stimuli, allowing them to peer into their planets to better understand why they do what they do. The perceptions in our planets of belief do not live in isolation, independent of our actions and interactions. We use them to interact with the world. If we can become more conscious of the shape and organization of our planets, we may become more powerful in the ways that we live our lives. As Carroll points out: 'We are not the reason for the existence of the universe, but our ability to self-awareness and reflection makes us special within it' (2016:161). That self-awareness is important in our daily workings because the more that we are aware of ourselves, the more that we can control what we do and how we do it. Being aware of the structures and connections of our beliefs, perceptions, stereotypes, and any other ideas we may have is the first step in changing how we interact with other people and what we get from the world.

Throughout this book, we use the findings from multiple studies in perceptual dialectology to show how the planets of belief metaphor is a strong visualization of the cognitive connection between language and other types of 'knowledge' (social traits, geography, etc.). We start with an overview of methods and studies in perceptual dialectology, and then we move through smaller and smaller frames of reference for the elicitation of beliefs – nation, region, and state – to show the strength of the metaphor – and perceptual dialectology – at any level. While the metaphor might be compatible with other theoretical and methodological approaches to language, we are focusing on perceptual dialectology for this book because of its inherent interest in attitudes, beliefs, and perceptions of language. We believe this approach has the potential to shift what people think, how they think, and why they stereotype others based on speech by making them consciously aware of the interaction between language use, perceptions, and stereotypes. That is, it gives us an opportunity to reinforce positive views of language and possibly change those that are hurtful.

References

Aarts, Henk, and A. P. Dijksterhuis. 2002. Category activation effects in judgment and behaviour: The moderating role of perceived comparability. *British Journal of Social Psychology* 41.123.

Altman, Irwin, and Dalmas A. Taylor. 1973. *Social penetration: The development of interpersonal relationships.* New York: Holt, Rinehart, & Winston.

Anisfeld, Moshe; Norman Bogo; and Wallace E. Lambert. 1962. Evaluational reactions to accented English speech. *Journal of Abnormal and Social Psychology* 65.4.223–31.

Babel, Anna M. (ed.) 2016. *Awareness and control in sociolinguistic research*. Cambridge: Cambridge University Press.

Bargh, John A., and Tanya L. Chartrand. 2000. Studying the mind in the middle: A practical guide to priming and automaticity research. *Handbook of research methods in social psychology*, ed. by H. Reis and C. Judd, 1–39. New York: Cambridge University Press.

Bassili, John, and Rick Brown. 2005. Implicit and explicit attitudes: Research, challenges, and theory. *Handbook of attitudes and attitude change*, ed. by Dolores Albarracin, Blair T. Johnson, and Mark P. Zanna. Mahwah, NJ: Lawrence Erlbaum Associates Publishers.

Bourdieu, Pierre. 1977. *Outline of a theory of practice*. Cambridge: Cambridge University Press.

Bourdieu, Pierre. 1990. Structures, habitus, practices. *The logic of practice*, ed. by Pierre Bourdieu, 52–65. Stanford, CA: Stanford University Press.

Burkette, Allison. 2016. *Language and material culture*. Amsterdam/Philadelphia, PA: John Benjamins.

Campbell-Kibler, Kathryn. 2016. Towards a cognitively realistic model of meaningful sociolinguistic variation. *Awareness and control in sociolinguistic research*, ed. by Anna Babel, 123–51. Cambridge: Cambridge University Press.

Carranza, Miguel A. 1982. Attitudinal research on Hispanic language varieties. *Attitudes towards language variation: Social and applied issues*, ed. by Ellen Bouchard Ryan and Howard Giles, 63–84. London, UK: Arnold.

Carroll, Sean. 2016. *The big picture: On the origins of life, meaning, and the universe itself.* New York: Penguin.

Cecil, Wes. 2019. Transevaluation of all values: Joy not fear. *YouTube*, January 18, 2019.

Cramer, Jennifer; Susan Tamasi; and Paulina Bounds. 2018. Southernness and our linguistic planets of belief: The view from Kentucky. *American Speech* 93.445–70.

Curzan, Anne, and Michael Adams. 2006. *How English works: A linguistic introduction*, 3rd edition. Boston, MA: Longman.

Day, Richard R. 1982. Children's attitudes toward language. *Attitudes towards language variation: Social and applied contexts*, ed. by Ellen Bouchard Ryan and Howard Giles, 116-131. London: Edward Arnold.

Dovidio, John F., and James M. Jones. 2019. Prejudice, stereotyping, and discrimination. *Advanced social psychology: The state of the science*, 2nd edition, ed. by E. J. Finkel and R. F. Baumeister, 3–23. Oxford: Oxford University Press.

Drager, Katie, and M. Joelle Kirtley. 2016. Awareness, salience, and stereotypes in exemplar-based models of speech production and perception. *Awareness and control in sociolinguistic research,* ed. by Anna Babel, 1–24. Cambridge: Cambridge University Press.

Eckert, Penelope. 2008. Variation and the indexical field. *Journal of Sociolinguistics* 12.4. 453–76.

Edwards, John. 1982. Language attitudes and their implication among English speakers. *Attitudes towards language variation*, ed. by Ellen Bouchard Ryan and Howard Giles, 20–33. London: Edward Arnold.

Edwards, John. 1999. Refining our understanding of language attitudes. *Journal of Language and Social Psychology* 18.1101–10.

Fausey, Caitlin, and Lera Boroditsky. 2011. Who dunnit? Cross-linguistic differences in eye-witness memory. *Psychonomic Bulletin & Review* 18.150–57.

Fishbein, Martin, and Bertram H. Raven. 1962. The AB scales: An operational definition of belief and attitude. *Human Relations* 15.35–44.

Flusberg, Stephen, and Lera Boroditsky. 2011. Are things that are hard to physically move also hard to imagine moving? *Psychonomic Bulletin & Review* 18.158–64.

Fought, Carmen. 2006. *Language and ethnicity.* New York: Cambridge University Press.

Fraser, Barry J. 1993. Incorporating classroom and school environment ideas into teacher education programs. *Teacher educators' annual handbook*, ed. by T. A. Simpson, 135–52. Brisbane, Australia: Queensland University of Technology.

Gardner, Robert, and Richard Clément. 1990. Social psychological perspectives on second language acquisition. *Handbook of language and social psychology*, ed. By W P. Robinson and Howard Giles. Hoboken, NJ: Wiley.

Giles, Howard; Chris Harrison; Clare Creber; Philip M. Smith; and Norman H. Freeman. 1983. Developmental and contextual aspects of children's language attitudes. *Language & Communication* 3.2.141–6.

Hartley, Laura C. 1999. A view from the West: Perceptions of U.S. dialects by Oregon residents. *The handbook of perceptual dialectology*, ed. by Dennis R. Preston. Philadelphia, PA: John Benjamins.

Irvine, Judith. 1989. When talk isn't cheap: Language and political economy. *American Ethnologist* 16.2.248–67.

Kahneman, Daniel. 2011. *Thinking, fast and slow.* New York: Farrar, Straus and Giroux.

Kolbert, Elizabeth. 2017. Why facts don't change our minds: New discoveries about the human mind show the limitations of reason. *The New Yorker.* https://www.newyorker.com/magazine/2017/02/27/why-facts-dont-change-our-minds.

Kramarae, Cheris. 1982. Women and men speaking: Framework for analysis. *Language* 58.4.940–3.

Kroskrity, Paul. 2004. Language ideologies. *Companion to linguistic anthropology*, ed. by Alessandro Duranti, 496–517. Malden, MA: Basil Blackwell.

Kretzschmar, William A., Jr. 2009. *The linguistics of speech.* Cambridge: Cambridge University Press.

Lakoff, George, and Mark Johnson. 1980. *Metaphors we live by.* Chicago, IL: University of Chicago Press.

Lambert, Wallace E. 1967. A social psychology of bilingualism. *Journal of Social Issues* 23.91–109.

Lambert, Wallace E.; R.C. Hodgsen; Robert C. Gardner; and Samuel Fillenbaum. 1960. Evaluational reactions to spoken languages. *Journal of Abnormal and Social Psychology* 60.44–51.

Lambert, Wallace; Moshe Anisfeld; and Grace Yeni-Komshian. 1965. Evaluational reactions of Jewish and Arab adolescents to dialect and language variations. *Journal of Personality and Social Psychology* 34.84–90. doi:10.1037/h0022088.

Lambert, Wallace E.; G. Richard Tucker; and Alison d'Anglejan. 1973. Cognitive and attitudinal consequences of bilingual schooling. *Journal of Educational Psychology* 65.2.141–59.

Lucy, John A. 1997. Linguistic relativity. *Annual Review of Anthropology* 26.291–312.

Lucy, John A. 2005. Through the window of language: Assessing the influence of language diversity on thought. *Theoria* 54.299–309.

Luhman, Reid. 1990. Appalachian English stereotypes: Language attitudes in Kentucky. *Language in Society* 19.331–48.

Macaulay, Ronald. 1977. *Language, social class and education: A Glasgow study.* Edinburgh: Edinburgh University Press.

Macnamara, John. 1973. Nurseries, streets and classrooms: Some comparisons and deductions. *The Modern Language Journal* 57.250–54.

Mandelbrot, Benoit. 1982. *The fractal geometry of nature.* San Francisco, CA: Freeman.

McGarty, Craig; Vincent Y. Yzerbyt; and Russell Spears. 2002. Social, cultural and cognitive factors in stereotype formation. *Stereotypes as explanations: The formation of meaningful beliefs about social groups*, ed. by Craig McGarty, Vincent Y. Yzerbyt, and Russell Spears, 1–16. Cambridge: Cambridge University Press.

McGowan, Kevin B. 2015. Social expectation improves speech perception in noise. *Language and Speech* 58.502–21.

Mercier, Hugo, and Dan Sperber. 2019. *Enigma of reason*. Cambridge: Harvard University Press.

Nehamas, Alexander. 1985. *Nietzsche: Life as literature*. Cambridge: Harvard University Press.

Preston, Dennis R. 1989. *Perceptual dialectology: Nonlinguists' views of areal linguistics*. Dordrecht, the Netherlands: Foris.

Preston, Dennis R. 2010. Variation in language regard. *Variatio delectat: Empirische Evidenzen und theoretische Passungen sprachlicher Variation* (für Klaus J. Mattheier zum 65. Geburtstag), ed. by E. Zeigler, P. Gilles, and J. Scharloth, 7–27. Frankfurt: Peter Lang.

Preston, Dennis R. 2016. Whaddayaknow now? *Awareness and control in sociolinguistic research*, ed. by A. Babel, 177–99. Cambridge: Cambridge University Press.

Preston, Dennis R. 2018. Language regard: What, why, how, whither. *Language regard: Methods, variation and change*, ed. by B.E. Evans, E.J. Benson, and J.N. Stanford, 3–28. Cambridge: Cambridge University Press.

Purnell, Thomas; William Idsardi; and John Baugh. 1999. Perceptual and phonetic experiments and American English dialect identification. *Journal of Language and Social Psychology* 18.10–30.

Roberts, Celia; Evelyn Davies; and Tom Jupp. 1992. *Language and discrimination*. London: Longman.

Rosenthal, Robert. 1974. *On the social psychology of the self-fulfilling prophecy: Further evidence for Pygmalion effects and their mediating mechanisms*. New York: MSS Modular Publications.

Ross, Lee, and Andrew Ward. 1995. Naive realism: Implications for misunderstanding and divergent perceptions of fairness and bias. *Values and knowledge*, ed. by T. Brown, E. Reed, and E. Turiel Hillsdale, 103–35. Hillsdale, NJ: Erlbaum.

Rubin, Donald L. 1992. Nonlanguage factors affecting undergraduates' judgments of nonnative English-speaking teaching assistants. *Research in Higher Education* 33.511–31.

Rubin, Donald L., and Kim A. Smith. 1990. Effects of accent, ethnicity, and lecture topic on undergraduates' perceptions of nonnative English-speaking teaching assistants. *International Journal of Intercultural Relations* 14.337–53.

Ryan, Ellen Bouchard. 1973. Subjective reactions toward accented speech. *Language attitudes*, ed. by Roger W. Shuy and Ralph W. Fasold, 60–73. Washington, DC: Georgetown University Press.

Ryan, Ellen Bouchard, and Miguel A. Carranza. 1975. Evaluative reactions of adolescents toward speakers of standard English and Mexican American accented English. *Journal of Personality and Social Psychology* 31.855–63. doi:10.1037/h0076704.

Ryan, Ellen Bouchard, and Howard Giles (eds.). 1982. *Attitudes towards language variation: Social and applied contexts*. London: Edward Arnold .

Sachs, J.; P. Lieberman; and D. Erickson. 1973. Anatomical and cultural determinants in male and female speech. *Language attitudes: Current trends and prospects*, ed. by Roger W. Shuy and Ralph W. Fasold, 74–83. Washington, DC: Georgetown University Press.

Sampson, P., and J. Palmer. 1973. The importance of being earnest about importance. *Market Research Society Conference*, 157–89.

Sapir, Edward. 1921. *Language: An introduction to the study of speech.* San Diego, CA: Harcourt, Brace.

Schön, Donald A. 1993. Generative metaphor: A perspective on problem setting in social policy. *Metaphor and thought,* ed. by A. Ortony, 137–63. Cambridge: Cambridge University Press.

Silverstein, Michael. 1979. Language structure and linguistic ideology. *The elements: A parasession on linguistic units and levels,* ed. by R. Clyne, W. Hanks, and C. Hofbauer, 293–47. Chicago, IL: Chicago Linguistic Society.

Squires, Lauren. 2016. Processing grammatical differences: Perceiving versus noticing. *Awareness and control in sociolinguistic research,* ed. by Anna Babel, 80–104. Cambridge: Cambridge University Press.

St. Clair, Robert N. 1982. From social history to language attitudes. *Attitudes toward language variation,* ed. by Ellen Bouchard Ryan and Howard Giles, 164–74. London: Edward Arnold.

Strand, Michael, and Omar Lizardo. 2015. Beyond world images: Belief as embodied action in the world. *Sociological Theory* 33.44–70.

Thibodeau, Paul, and Lera Boroditsky. 2011. Metaphors we think with: The role of metaphor in reasoning. *PLoS ONE* 6.e16782(1-10).

Thibodeau, Paul, and Lera Boroditsky. 2015. Measuring effects of metaphor in a dynamic opinion landscape. *PLos ONE* 10.e0133939(1-22).

Uleman, James S., and John A. Bargh (eds.) 1989. *Unintended thought.* New York: The Guilford Press.

Whorf, Benjamin. 1941. The relation of habitual thought and behavior to language. *Language, culture, and personality: Essays in memory of Edward Sapir,* ed. by Leslie Spier, 75–93. Menasha, WI: Sapir Memorial Publication Fund.

Wölck, Wolfgang. 1973. Attitudes towards Spanish and Quechua in bilingual Peru. *Language attitudes: Current trends and prospects,* ed. by Roger W. Shuy and Ralph W. Fasold, 129–47. Washington, DC: Georgetown UP.

Wolff, Phillip, and Kevin Holmes. 2010. *Linguistic relativity.* Hoboken, NJ: John Wiley & Sons, Ltd.

Woolard, Kathryn. 1992. Language ideology: Issues and approaches. *Pragmatics* 2.3.235–49.

2

PERCEPTUAL DIALECTOLOGY AND THE POWER OF LABELING

Introduction

In thinking about the metaphor of planets of belief that was introduced in the previous chapter and the interconnected ways in which human perception links with attitudes, beliefs, reactions, and the like, we find language to be a fertile testing ground for its application. In particular, the linguistic study of the perceptions nonlinguists hold about language variation and change, known as PERCEPTUAL DIALECTOLOGY (e.g. Preston 1989; Cramer & Montgomery 2016), allows for the systematic analysis of this type of interconnectedness by examining nonlinguists' explicit beliefs about language and linguistic variation. In this chapter, we describe this subfield of linguistics, including its data collection, processing, and analysis procedures. We also highlight how, in completing a map drawing task in which nonlinguists indicate the linguistic varieties they perceive in a given geographic space, the production of labels for those linguistic varieties has been essentially overlooked within the research conducted using this approach. By providing a description of the research paradigm most commonly employed in this subfield, we lay the foundation for understanding the analyses of perceptual dialectology data that are presented in the following chapters.

A history of perceptual dialectology

American linguistics has a long history of being generally uninterested in non-production-based linguistic data. The development of the field as a whole in the United States, and of dialect study in particular, has strong ties to structuralist paradigms (cf. Bloomfield 1944) that essentially ignored language attitudes in favor of 'real' data, most notably the grammatical, lexical, and phonetic variables commonly studied within these traditions.

In many traditional dialectology studies, such as those that seek to define dialect regions using lexical data (e.g. responses to the prompt 'What do you call a carbonated beverage?') or phonetic data (e.g. whether an informant pronounces *pin* and *pen* the same), the inclusion of overt beliefs about linguistic variation is almost completely absent. In the 1960s, however, Hoenigswald ignited interest in the study of these beliefs, contending that

> we should be interested not only in (a) what goes on (language), but also in (b) how people react to what goes on (they are persuaded, they are put off, etc.) and in (c) what people say goes on (talk concerning language). It will not do to dismiss these secondary and tertiary modes of conduct merely as sources of error.
>
> (1966:20)

This call to action is often cited as the beginning of what might be called modern FOLK LINGUISTICS, a term that encompasses the many ways of examining the beliefs that nonlinguists hold about language. Perceptual dialectology is one such area that

> seeks to include what nonlinguists think about linguistic practices, including where they think variation comes from, where they think it exists, and why they think it happens, in holistic examinations of variation that incorporate aspects of both linguistic production and perception.
>
> (Cramer 2016a:1)

Preston (e.g. 1989) answered Hoenigswald's call, developing the methods that are most commonly used in perceptual dialectology today, emphasizing and extrapolating on the idea that what people say (language production) activates both conscious and unconscious reactions (language perception). Preston expanded upon the components listed in Hoenigswald's call and represented them visually, as in Figure 2.1.

Within perceptual dialectology as a field of inquiry, the methods researchers employ today to gain such a multifaceted understanding of how nonlinguists view their dialect landscapes draw heavily on the early work of Preston. These methods typically include (Preston 1999:xxxiv):

1. The *Draw-a-map* task: participants are given a map of a specified geographic territory with minimal detail (in the United States, maps typically contain only state boundaries; see Bounds and Sutherland 2018 for a discussion of the importance of basemap selection) and are asked to indicate where on the map they perceive certain ways of speaking; participants are also asked to label each region that they indicate.
2. The *Degree-of-difference rating* task: given some set of entities (e.g. states, cities, countries, regions identified in the mapping task), participants are asked to

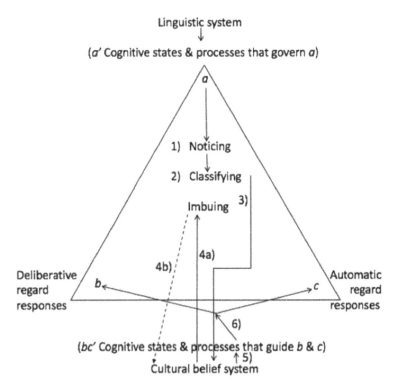

Linguistic system

(*a′* Cognitive states & processes that govern *a*)

a

1) Noticing

2) Classifying

Imbuing   3)

4a)

4b)   *b*   *c*

Deliberative regard responses

Automatic regard responses

6)

(*bc′* Cognitive states & processes that guide *b* & *c*)   ↑ 5)

Cultural belief system

FIGURE 2.1   Connections between language use and perceptions of language use (based on Preston 2010). Source: Courtesy of Niedzielski & Preston (2020: 97).

rank the linguistic variety they associate with each entity with respect to its perceived level of difference from the participant's own way of speaking.

3. The *Pleasantness* and *Correctness rating* task: as with the degree-of-difference task, participants are given a set of entities and are asked to rate each one, this time with respect to how pleasant or how correct they perceive that entity's speech to be; in some research (e.g. Cramer 2016b; Tamasi 2003), entities have been rated for additional social attributes (e.g. education, formality, beauty) as well.

4. The *Dialect identification* task: participants listen to speech samples and are asked to identify the place from which they believe the voice comes.

5. *Qualitative data analysis*: researchers in perceptual dialectology also rely on sociolinguistic interviews with the participants who take part in the tasks described above and on discourse analysis of these interviews; such open-ended conversations reveal a wealth of information about the sentiments that participants hold about language, dialects, and variation, as well as the speakers who use certain varieties.

Ultimately, these tools (and extrapolations of these tools) have been utilized in various studies, including full country, regional, and state-based analyses in the US (e.g. Preston 1989; Benson 2003; Tamasi 2003; Hartley 2005; Fridland & Bartlett 2006; Bucholtz et al. 2007, 2008; Evans 2011; Cukor-Avila et al. 2012; Jones 2015; Cramer 2016b) and in countless locations around the globe (e.g. Kuiper 1999; Dailey-O'Cain 1999; Diercks 2002; Montgomery 2007, 2016; Bounds 2015; Braber 2016; Jeon & Cukor-Avila 2016). Together, these tools and analyses have provided a well-rounded view of the perceptions held by nonlinguists about linguistic variation in given locales. Such information reveals

> not only a representation of where [participants] believe the physical boundaries of certain varieties exist but also ratings of, accuracy of identification of, and their qualitative beliefs and attitudes toward the varieties they perceive. Such a methodology allows researchers to go beyond the question of whether differences are perceived between varieties in order to systematically examine how those perceptions are operationalized.
>
> (Cramer 2016a:6)

Despite the importance of his early studies in the field, Preston is quick to point out that his work was not the beginning of perceptual dialectology, and he cites several researchers in the Netherlands and Japan who were doing similar work even before Hoenigswald's call (Preston 1999). In the Netherlands, Rensink (1955, reprinted in Preston 1999) asked research participants to identify areas of the country that were similar to and different from their own linguistic varieties, utilizing the 'little-arrow method' (Weijnen 1946) to link 'a respondent's home area to another that the respondent asserts to be linguistically similar to the locations they described as linguistically similar' (Preston 1999:xxvi). In Japan, at essentially the same time but without knowledge of the little-arrow method, Sibata (1959, reprinted in Preston 1999) asked participants to name places that spoke varieties that were different from their own. The analysis of this data involved delineating dialect areas by separating towns and villages by lines of differing thicknesses to indicate more or less similarity between them.

These early studies showed that the perceptions of nonlinguists sometimes align with production maps of linguistic variation, while at other times they do not. This mismatch was acknowledged as a potential outcome of perceptual dialectology studies in Benson (2003), in which she said,

> Studies in perceptual dialectology need not be used only to confirm or contradict production boundaries. Indeed, studies in perceptual dialectology can inform our understanding of the criteria that are important to the folk in defining dialect regions and should be considered in the construction of dialect maps.
>
> (307)

For researchers in Japan, however, the mismatch between perceptual and production boundaries was seen as troubling, leading Sibata to call his own data uninteresting. From our perspective, the mismatch itself is what is interesting, and in recent research (e.g. Cramer 2016b) it has even served as the reason for exploring the perception data in and of itself. Nonetheless, early researchers in this area essentially abandoned the cause because of the mismatch, instead of seeing it as a catalyst for further study.

Preston saw the controversy in the Netherlands and Japan as indicative of the need to understand these perceptions, so as to understand the production data more fully. In more than three decades of research within this paradigm, Preston has made it clear why the study of language regard, or the overarching area that considers attitudes, beliefs, and ideologies as the cornerstone of understanding language use, is so important to our work as linguists:

> Occasionally studies of language regard do not fare well in the court of professional opinion. 'Who cares what people think and feel? We're (socio) linguists and want to know what they do' [...] 'thinking' and 'feeling' are not only modes of 'doing' but are also inextricably entwined with the better-recognized 'doings' of language production and perception.
>
> (Preston 2018:4)

It would be an overstatement to suggest that perceptual dialectology is the only area of study concerned with linguistic perceptions. Sociolinguistics, the larger subfield into which perceptual dialectology and these other fields are placed, has emphasized the impact of beliefs and attitudes for much of its history, including early work by Labov (1972) with African Americans in New York City, making connections between language use and language attitudes. Many such studies, however, have not been focused on the overt opinions of nonlinguists; this wealth of information about covert beliefs is important and extends work completed within the traditions of sociology of language (e.g. Fishman et al. 1971) and social psychology (e.g. Lambert et al. 1960; Ryan & Giles 1982). Perceptual dialectology makes the leap to the examination of overt attitudes and reactions to language, and, as such, serves as a linguistic subfield uniquely suited to the application of the planets of belief metaphor. In what follows, we focus specifically on how mental map data and the labels employed by nonlinguists in performing this task can begin to reveal these planets, discussing the importance of such data for our broader understanding of linguistic perception.

Maps and labels

To understand how perceptions are elicited in perceptual dialectology research, it is best to start with an example. Our focus in this book is on the draw-a-map task described above, and the image in Figure 2.2 is an example of a map collected in conducting the research project that served as the basis of Cramer (2016b). Please note that our respondent hand-drawn maps have been redrawn for clarity; original spelling and punctuation have been retained. This

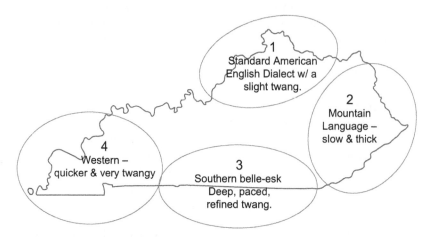

FIGURE 2.2   Map drawn by an 18-year-old female from Lexington, KY.

map features four perceived dialect regions: 'Standard American English Dialect w/ a slight twang'; 'Mountain Language – slow & thick'; 'Southern belle-esk Deep, paced, refined twang'; and 'Western – quicker & very twangy'.

There are several things to note about this map and these labels. The participant was handed a simple outline of the state of Kentucky with no other details given. The amount of territory provided seems to condition how much detail is offered by the map drawer, such that participants given a map that includes Kentucky as well as its surrounding areas draw fewer divisions within the state than they do when just given a map of the state (see Cramer 2016b). Also, even early work in perceptual dialectology (e.g. Preston 1989, 1996) suggested that people tend to draw the most stigmatized areas first, followed by additional details for their home areas. In full US studies, the most commonly drawn region is the Southern region, likely because of the salience of its stigmatization across the country (Preston 1996). Within Kentucky, the most stigmatized region is the Appalachian region, located in the eastern portion of the state and represented on this map in the region called 'Mountain Language – slow & thick'. It is not, however, the only stigmatized area; as you will note, the descriptors given for each region aside from the Appalachian one include the word 'twang', a term that is generally used pejoratively by Americans referring to accents that have some Southern association. Indeed, Kentucky speech is variously subjected to negative ideologies about Southernness, even among Kentuckians.

In terms of these ideologies, this map creator rated the region 'Standard American English Dialect w/ a slight twang' as least different from her own, despite the fact that the home area she lists is Lexington, an area not encompassed by any region she has drawn. This 'no man's land' effect is common in such studies, especially in full country studies. It is assumed, in these cases, that the participant simply has no specific knowledge of the region or does not associate a specific way of speaking with it. It is also possible that leaving an area without designation indicates that the area is 'unmarked' linguistically, meaning that the participant sees this area as 'standard' or 'normal' (that is, respondents may see this region as the place where people 'don't have accents'). However, many participants feel a need to cover every corner of a given area, which can result in some geographically incorrect responses (e.g. mislabeled states, confused cardinal directions). Plus, drawing a region simply to fill a space does not necessarily mean that a person holds any specific ideologies about that place. There was a similar effect in many pleasantness and correctness rating tasks in which participants were asked to rate all 50 US states; even if participants knew nothing about a state, they would rate it. While the point of perceptual dialectology research is to elicit real perceptions, researchers must be wary of the desire of participants to simply finish the task.

This same issue of forced responses was also seen in the pile sort maps used in Tamasi (2003). Instead of using Preston's draw-a-map method, participants in Tamasi's study were asked to create dialect boundaries using a pile sort, a method developed by anthropologists to investigate the cultural organization of folk knowledge. Participants were given a stack of 50 index cards, each with a state name printed on it, and were asked to sort the cards into piles where people speak similarly versus differently from one another. This technique removes the spatial component of traditional map tasks and requires participants to use only their own beliefs about language in their decision-making process. In constructing their dialect regions, participants were allowed to make any number of piles and place as many cards in each pile as they felt necessary. Additionally, respondents were instructed to 'think aloud' as they worked, in order for researchers to collect additional information that the participants used in constructing their responses. Even though respondents were not specifically working with a map, one was available for them to consult. While geography remained the prime factor in the division of states by dialect region, this method allowed for other factors, such as perceptions of pleasantness and industriousness, to appear as inherently connected to concepts of space. In fact, the requirement of categorizing all 50 states seemed to not affect participant responses as much as it did when respondents tried to cover the entire map space in draw-a-map tasks, because they were able to simultaneously reference other associated information as well.

Returning to the perceptions provided as part of the map in Figure 2.2, this participant's ratings were not as telling as those from other respondents. Aside from marking all other regions except 'Standard American English Dialect w/ a slight twang' as 'different' from her own, she rated them all similarly in terms of correctness, pleasantness, and beauty. She rated the eastern Kentucky region as 'nonstandard' and 'informal'. In addition to the numerical ratings, participants were also asked to provide qualitative responses to the following questions: 'How else might you describe this way of speaking?'; 'Why did you select this label for this way of speaking?'; and 'What does this label mean to you?' The participant used words like 'Redneck' and 'very twangy' to describe the western Kentucky variety, while she reports the variety in the northern part of the state as having '[n]ot as much character as other KY dialects, but not lacking either', claiming it is '[v]ery close to O[hio] dialect but still Kentuckian'. This description, along with the label, which also highlights the idea that the participant sees it as standard 'w/ a slight twang', is further evidence of the border nature of Kentucky. Cramer (2016b) showed that Kentuckians, and Louisvillians in particular, see Kentucky as a place between places (Llamas 2007).

Maps and labels in this Kentucky-centered research show similarities to those found in other perceptual dialectology studies. Evans (2016), in exploring the terms *country* and *gangster* in Washington, finds a rural–urban divide that is similar to the one described in Cramer's work (e.g. Cramer 2016c). The map Evans gave participants differed in that it was not only an outline of the state but also showed where major cities and highways were, to aid the participants in their geographic understanding. This study, as well as others carried out by Evans and her team, has revealed a dichotomy that, while very clear in the American South, seems perhaps less likely in the Pacific Northwest. Labels like 'hick', 'rednecks', and 'farmers' appear in the eastern part of the state, on the other side of the 'Cascade Curtain', a local term that Evans (2013a) deploys to describe the rather strong effect that the Cascade Mountains have as a perceptual linguistic border in the state, from the more urban western areas of Seattle and Tacoma, where participants used labels like 'ghetto', 'gangster', and 'gang talk'. What is perhaps most interesting about the rural–urban divide exhibited in these (and other) perceptual dialectology studies is that even though sociologists (e.g. Lichter & Brown 2011) indicate that rural–urban divides are an obsolete way of viewing society, the distinction remains an important classification system for nonlinguists describing their dialect landscapes.

Ultimately, the combination of maps and labels looks like a map of an individual's language ideologies. If we want to learn more about the speech community's ideologies, we have to combine the individual maps into composite maps. Figure 2.3 is an example of a composite map created to highlight how Louisvillians perceive their place in the dialect landscape of this smaller region of the United States (Cramer 2016b). This map was created by layering all the individual maps collected in the community, using the tools of geographic information systems (GIS) to digitize each region and create an agreement level representation that, in this case, shows where at least 50% of participants agree on the location of a specific dialect area (see Montgomery & Stoeckle 2013 and Montgomery & Cramer 2016 for more on the use of GIS in perceptual dialectology research). Some participants drew larger regions and others smaller ones, but the space covered by the single area represented on the map in the composite indicates the area that is most likely the location of the dialect under analysis.

But how do perceptual dialectologists decide what to represent on these maps? Preston (1989) arbitrarily chose to represent regions that appeared on at least five participant maps. Cramer (2016b) followed suit and only included regions that appeared on 14% of the maps (a number devised by computing the

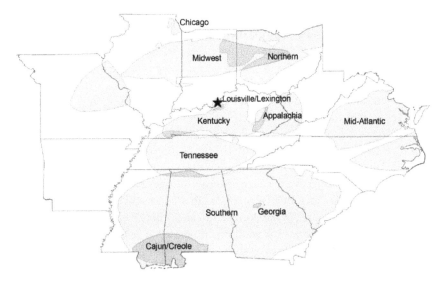

FIGURE 2.3 50% agreement composite map for Louisvillians.

percentage in Preston's work, in which five maps represented about 14% of the 35 maps collected in that study). In these and numerous other perceptual dialectology studies, the answer is that, despite the value in the bottom-up approach to dialect region labeling on the part of the participant, analysis of this kind of data requires the researcher to make certain decisions and assumptions that would not be required in studies where participants do not have free choice of labels.

The necessary insertion of the researcher is most clear when it comes to deciding that 'the same region' is represented on more than one map. In one case, two different participants use the same label, let's say 'Midwest', but they include completely different geographical spaces within the regions for which they use this label. Perhaps one person's 'Midwest' centers on Ohio, while the other person's on Illinois. If the researcher decides to call these the same, this will potentially result in disjointed composite regions like the one for 'Midwest' in Figure 2.3. In another case, two different participants use different labels, let's say 'Appalachian' and 'Mountain', but they have included very similar geographic territory in the enclosed region. If the researcher decides to call these the same, that researcher will need to choose an overarching category label to subsume them. Preston (1989:27) provided a generic template with geographical indications for various, neutrally named American English dialect regions, including entities like 'New England' and 'Southwest'. The template does not, however, include the breadth of variation that participants in Cramer (2016b) wanted to indicate. For example, Preston did not include an Appalachian area in his template, and this region was one of the most commonly delimited areas for Kentuckians. So geographic region and frequency of occurrence are both important aspects of determining the categories to be represented.

The researcher must also consider how these linguistic entities are represented in the research products. Many labels given by participants are derogatory, and researchers may need to consider, in creating composite maps, what entity is being referenced by labels like 'hillbilly', 'hick', and 'redneck', words that are generally negative markers for Appalachianness, Southernness, and/or rurality. In this book, it is these kinds of labels – the individual, participant-selected labels – in which we are most interested. Figure 2.4, for example, shows the overlay of all regions drawn in Kentucky with the labels 'hillbilly', 'hick', and 'redneck' (Cramer, Tamasi, & Bounds 2018). Interestingly, map drawers did not use these labels when referencing the speech of Louisville, the state's largest city, represented in the map by a star. But every single other corner of the state was touched at least once by these labels. What does this mean for how Kentuckians as a whole perceive variation in the state? What do their planets of belief look like?

Finally, as we mentioned previously, many participants feel the need to cover an entire map, while others leave places uncovered. Those who insist on including every portion of a geographic area within some dialect region often produce labels that occur infrequently (Bounds & Cramer 2017). Such labels are often excluded from analysis; other data are excluded in these studies when: participants do not complete the task fully or correctly (Evans 2013b), the data fails to meet a threshold in the analysis procedure (Preston 1989; Cramer 2016b), or the labels do not neatly fit into some defined semantic category (see above). Bounds and Cramer (2017) found national-level labels like 'Do people live here?' primarily used to describe the Great Plains area of the United States, indicating the desire to cover the entire country but also showcasing a complete lack of knowledge about the people of the Great Plains and their language use. Additionally, in examining regional- and state-level data, Bounds and Cramer showed a desire to represent entities not on the map, such as nearby states (Jones & Cramer 2017), or

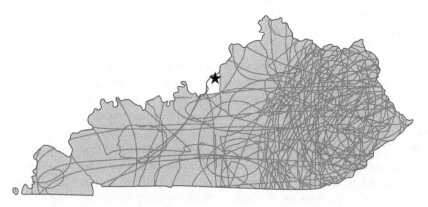

FIGURE 2.4 All regions marked as 'hillbilly', 'hick', or 'redneck' in Kentucky. Source: Courtesy of Cramer, Tamasi, & Bounds (2018).

entities not easily amenable to mapping, like African American English. These infrequent labels still exhibit the ideologies present, even when the map has areas that participants have no knowledge of. That is, when the map does not have what participants know, or when they do not know what is on the map, they still feel the need to express some metalinguistic commentary. We tend to exclude these infrequent labels as data in perceptual dialectology studies because they do not reflect larger ideologies than those of the individual. However, in using the metaphor of planets of belief as a tool for engaging with these data in new ways, we believe even these infrequent labels can provide important information about nonlinguists' language worldview. The map itself, as well as the labeling process, is playing a role in conditioning not only perceptions but also belief planets.

Perceptual dialectology planets

Once we recognize that our perceptions about everything inform us, guide us, push us, and even command us in countless ways, we can recognize the power that perception holds for our lives. With language, too, it seems that what we think about it – how it is used, how it is 'supposed to be' used, how we think people use it, what the people who use certain varieties are like – impacts what we do in our day-to-day lives of interacting with other language users. Preston was aware of this impact, and he urged linguists to grapple with perceptions in their work because

> [w]ithout knowledge of the value-ridden classifications of language and language status and function by the folk, without knowledge of where the folk believe differences exist, without knowledge of where they are capable of hearing major and minor differences, and, most importantly, without knowledge of how the folk bring their beliefs about language to bear on their solutions to linguistic problems, the study of language attitudes risks being: 1) a venture into the investigation of academic distinctions which distort the folk reality or tell only a partial truth or, worse, 2) a misadventure into the study of theatrically exaggerated speech caricatures.
>
> (1993:252)

We are arguing here that these beliefs, however, are often below the level of consciousness, as represented in Figure 2.1. With language ideologies circulating as a form of internal knowledge for individuals, linguists must find ways of making such beliefs explicit. Perceptual dialectology provides the right tools and methodologies for extracting these internal beliefs. And despite the fact that individual ideologies are simply the ideologies of an individual, the vast majority of research in this tradition shows that there are many similarities among individuals within a community. Why might this be?

If we return to the map in Figure 2.2, we see that the individual used the word 'twang' in several of her descriptions. This word has a dictionary definition, which prioritizes the musical sense of the word, and a colloquial definition, which references a nasal voice quality that might be imitative of the musical sound, but it does not really have a technical definition for linguists separate from this folk notion (e.g. Montgomery 2008). However, it is a term that shows up again and again in perceptual dialectology maps. It appears so much that Preston, giving participants several characteristics on a scale (e.g., *slow–fast*, *smart–dumb*, *friendly–unfriendly*), included twang–no twang as a pairing for his Michigan respondents, who rated the North and South almost as polar opposites, such that having a twang, being casual and down-to-earth, and speaking slowly were attributes of Southernness, while being smart, normal, and educated were attributes of the North (and Michigan specifically). Of these results, Preston said, 'This is not very surprising, considering well-known folk and popular culture attitudes' (Preston 2002:56).

While well known, it has been shown that concepts like 'twang' are difficult to define, even for those willing to attach the label to a given group. Oxley (2015) cites typical connections of 'twang' to rurality, Southernness, and the (social and linguistic) stereotypes that coincide with the two. But the term also shows up in descriptions of speech in Ohio, Indiana, and other parts of the Midwest (Benson 2003), in Evans' (2011) work in Washington, and in parts of California (Bucholtz et al. 2007) as well. Indeed, the concept is so unclear, Rodgers (2016) undertook an entire study to flesh out the nuances of 'twang' as a perceptual term used to describe speech in Oklahoma. Her work showed that the term 'has a complex socioindexical profile characterized by several value dimensions revealed in the local, rhetorical, and interactional contexts of ideological constructions of social group identities and dialect differences in American English' (Rodgers 2016:416).

This is where the planets of belief metaphor is very useful. In Figure 2.5, we have a visualization of what a belief planet might look like with respect to the notion of 'twang'. In it, thicker lines indicate the most likely concepts

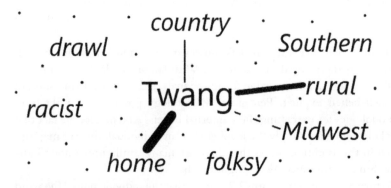

FIGURE 2.5 Potential belief planet around 'twang'.

to be connected to 'twang' for an individual. Thinner lines represent more tenuous connections (i.e. the person recognizes the potential connection, but it is less likely to be automatically triggered), dashed lines represent uncertain connections (i.e. they have heard this connection, but they don't necessarily agree with it), and the other characteristics form the cloud of disconnected notions that are not activated for this individual when they hear or use the word 'twang'. Maybe this belief planet belongs to an Oklahoman who thinks their own speech and that of their family is a 'twang'. They see it (and themselves) as rural and potentially country, but they would never characterize it (or themselves) as Southern or Midwestern, even though they know people talk about 'Midwestern twangs'.

When this hypothetical person fills out a perceptual dialectology map task, they might circle their home region and use the word 'twang' as a descriptor. Furthermore, it would not be unlikely that others from their community might use the word in the same way. This is where shared experience comes into play. The fact that 'twang' and its many similar notions co-occur in perceptual dialectology project after perceptual dialectology project indicates some larger shared (stereotypical) understanding of the term. The term circulates beyond this individual; it is present, with specific, associated imagery, in Hollywood, in art and music, in the news and social media, and in everyday, in-person conversation. What would be unlikely is for a person who used the word 'twang' to connect it to other things, like vanity, swift running, and good comedic timing. But such connections are not impossible, and understanding how individuals make these connections between what they perceive in their linguistic worlds and the labels, descriptions, and attitudes they attribute to entities in those worlds is important for a better understanding not only of language but also of the social, psychological, and cognitive realities of being a language user in a language-using world.

Perceptual dialectology research allows us to elicit these ideas about belief planets, and not only through the map drawing and labeling task. When we ask our subjects to rate and describe these dialect areas, we are explicitly asking them to confront their belief planets. Most people, as the metaphor would suggest, are unfazed by this task. They simply list their language ideologies, completing the task at hand, and continue with their potentially problematic ideas about language, language use, and language users. Their planet is coherent and impenetrable. If they are holding on to an ideology that is problematic, however, they may feel the need to address it. For example, in numerous instances where the label selected was perceived by the participant as potentially pejorative (e.g. 'hillbilly', 'redneck'), participants in Cramer (2016b) commented on this fact explicitly, saying that they were aware that such labels were stereotypical, as they did not necessarily pertain to all people in an area, and were possibly overly negative. This recognition indicates that those completing the task in this way reflected on their own perceptions. This is the power of perceptual dialectology.

Understanding linguistic perception

As we described in the first chapter, other models of perception exist in linguistics. These various understandings of language regard (Preston 2010), awareness and control (Babel 2016), and others have paved the way for engaging with cognitive models and psychological realities in understanding how nonlinguists think about language and linguistic variation. Perceptual dialectology is another way of examining these same kinds of beliefs, in an explicit and overt way, and it has the potential to reveal much about the ways that people construct their linguistic planets of belief. The research presented in the rest of this book showcases the ways in which the construction of belief planets is intimately entangled with our notions of identity. For example, we will showcase, as we did in Cramer, Tamasi, and Bounds (2018:21), how 'Kentuckians appear to hold a view something like "I'm Southern, but not *that* type of Southern" or perhaps "Southern isn't bad but rural is"'.

The chapters that follow take the theory and methods of perceptual dialectology and combine them with the power of understanding provided by the planets of belief metaphor to examine national-, regional-, state-, and local-level perceptions of language. The results of these examinations are varied; as indicated earlier, the scope of the geography is important. In national- and regional-level perceptions, participants tend to rely more on superficial stereotypes than on any detailed descriptions. When we zoom into state- and local-level perceptions, we see exactly how granular our planets of belief can be. When these lower-level perceptions are compared to higher-level ones, participants make more nuanced distinctions.

As the larger focus of the book is on data collected in Kentucky, Tennessee, and Georgia (though not exclusively), we will engage with the notion of Southernness. What is perhaps most interesting about the belief planets that we will explore is that participants from three states that are all ostensibly Southern have differing views on what constitutes 'real' Southern. It appears that our regional experiences can have contrasting and even contradicting impacts on the language ideologies we present. And these views change as the geographic scope of the map changes as well (e.g. national- vs. regional- vs. state-based research projects, as presented here).

Once we have examined these various levels of perception, we return to the planets of belief metaphor once more. We hope that the data, methods, theories, and metaphors presented in this book do more than simply highlight the patterns present in these linguistic beliefs. We hope to show that the words, sounds, and structures we use, the way these words, sounds, and structures are perceived, and the way that language interacts with society, both in the macro and the micro, are intimately entangled, and the way nonlinguists talk about linguistic variation can have an impact on a person's self-worth. In the end, our goal is to explicitly encourage readers to carefully consider the negative perceptions they carry about people and their linguistic varieties, and to destroy those planets of belief that cause others harm.

References

Babel, Anna M. (ed.) 2016. *Awareness and control in sociolinguistic research*. Cambridge: Cambridge University Press.

Benson, Erica J. 2003. Folk linguistic perceptions and the mapping of dialect boundaries. *American Speech* 78.307–30.

Bloomfield, Leonard. 1944. Secondary and tertiary responses to language. *Language* 20.45–55.

Bounds, Paulina. 2015. Perceptual regions in Poland. *Journal of Linguistic Geography* 3.34–45.

Bounds, Paulina, and Jennifer Cramer. 2017. Labels as outliers. *Paper presented at Diversity and Variation in Language (DiVar 1)*, Atlanta, GA, as part of the panel "Linguistic Planets of Belief and the American South".

Bounds, Paulina, and Charles J. Sutherland. 2018. Perceptual basemaps reloaded: The role basemaps play in eliciting perceptions. *Journal of Linguistic Geography* 6.145–66.

Braber, Natalie. 2016. Dialect perception and identification in Nottingham.*Cityscapes and perceptual dialectology: Global perspectives on non-linguists' knowledge of the dialect landscape*, ed. by Jennifer Cramer and Chris Montgomery, 209–31. Berlin: Mouton de Gruyter.

Bucholtz, Mary; Nancy Bermudez; Victor Fung; Lisa Edwards; and Rosalva Vargas. 2007. Hella Nor Cal or totally so Cal?: The perceptual dialectology of California. *Journal of English Linguistics* 35.325–52.

Bucholtz, Mary; Nancy Bermudez; Victor Fung; Rosalva Vargas; and Lisa Edwards. 2008. The normative North and the stigmatized South: Ideology and methodology in the perceptual dialectology of California. *Journal of English Linguistics* 36.62–87.

Cramer, Jennifer. 2016a. Perceptual dialectology. *Oxford Handbooks Online*. Retrieved 1 Jul. 2019, from https://www.oxfordhandbooks.com/view/10.1093/oxfordhb/9 780199935345.001.0001/oxfordhb-9780199935345-e-60.

Cramer, Jennifer. 2016b. *Contested southernness: The linguistic production and perception of identities in the borderlands*. Publication of the American Dialect Society 100. Durham, NC: Duke University Press.

Cramer, Jennifer. 2016c. Rural vs. urban: Perception and production of identity in a border city. ed. by Jennifer Cramer and Chris Montgomery, 27–54. Berlin: Mouton de Gruyter.

Cramer, Jennifer, and Chris Montgomery (eds.) 2016. *Cityscapes and perceptual dialectology: Global perspectives on non-linguists' knowledge of the dialect landscape*. Berlin: Mouton de Gruyter.

Cramer, Jennifer; Susan Tamasi; and Paulina Bounds. 2018. Southernness and our linguistic planets of belief. *American Speech* 93.445–70.

Cukor-Avila, Patricia; Lisa Jeon; Patricia C. Rector; Chetan Tiwari; and Zak Shelton. 2012. Texas – It's like a whole nuther country: Mapping Texans' perceptions of dialect variation in the Lone Star state. *Proceedings from the Twentieth Annual Symposium about Language and Society*, Austin, TX: Texas Linguistics Forum.

Dailey-O'Cain, Jennifer. 1999. The perception of post-unification German regional speech. *Handbook of perceptual dialectology*, vol. 1, ed. by Dennis Preston, 227–42. Amsterdam: John Benjamins.

Diercks, Willy. 2002. Mental maps: Linguistic-geographic concepts. *Handbook of perceptual dialectology*, vol. 2, ed. by D. Long and D. Preston, 51–70. Amsterdam: John Benjamins.

Evans, Betsy E. 2011. Seattletonian to faux hick: Mapping perceptions of English in WA. *American Speech* 86.383–413.

Evans, Betsy E. 2013a. Seattle to Spokane: Mapping perceptions of English in WA. *Journal of English Linguistics* 41.268–91.

Evans, Betsy E. 2013b. 'Everybody sounds the same': Otherwise overlooked ideology in perceptual dialectology. *American Speech* 88.63–80.

Evans, Betsy E. 2016. City talk and country talk: Perceptions of urban and rural English in Washington state. *Cityscapes and perceptual dialectology: Global perspectives on non-linguists' knowledge of the dialect landscape*, ed. by J. Cramer & C. Montgomery, 55–72. Berlin: Mouton de Gruyter.

Fishman, Joshua A.; Robert L. Cooper; and Roxanna Ma. 1971. *Bilingualism in the barrio* (Language Science Monographs No. 7). Bloomington, IN: Research Center in Anthropology, Folklore and Linguistics.

Fridland, Valerie, and Kathryn Bartlett. 2006. Correctness, pleasantness, and degree of difference ratings across regions. *American Speech* 81.358–86.

Hartley, Laura C. 2005. The consequences of conflicting stereotypes: Bostonian perceptions of U.S. dialects. *American Speech* 80.388–405.

Hoenigswald, Henry. 1966. A proposal for the study of folk-linguistics. *Sociolinguistics*, ed. by W. Bright, 116–26. The Hague: Mouton de Gruyter.

Jeon, Lisa, and Patricia Cukor-Avila. 2016. Urbanicity and language variation and change: Mapping dialect perceptions in and of Seoul. *Cityscapes and perceptual dialectology: Global perspectives on non-linguists' knowledge of the dialect landscape*, ed. by Jennifer Cramer and Chris Montgomery, 97–116. Berlin: Mouton de Gruyter.

Jones, Benjamin G. 2015. *Perceptual dialectology of New England: Views from Maine and the Web*. Lexington, KY: University of Kentucky Master's thesis.

Jones, Benjamin G., and Jennifer Cramer. 2017. Maps and proximity effects: The salience of neighboring locales on region- and state-level maps in perceptual dialectology. *Poster presented at the annual meeting of the American Dialect Society*, Austin, TX.

Kuiper, Lawrence. 1999. Variation and the norm: Parisian perceptions of regional France. *Handbook of perceptual dialectology*, vol. 1, ed. by Dennis Preston, 243–62. Amsterdam: John Benjamins.

Labov, William. 1972. *Language in the inner city*. Philadelphia, PA: University of Pennsylvania Press.

Lambert, Wallace E.; R.C. Hodgsen; R.C. Gardner; and S. Fillenbaum. 1960. Evaluational reactions to spoken language. *Journal of Abnormal and Social Psychology* 60.44–51.

Lichter, Daniel T., and David L. Brown. 2011. Rural America in an urban society: Changing spatial and social boundaries. *Annual Review of Sociology* 37.565–92.

Llamas, Carmen. 2007. 'A place between places': Language and identities in a border town. *Language in Society* 36.579–604.

Montgomery, Chris. 2007. *Northern English dialects: A perceptual approach*. Sheffield, UK: University of Sheffield PhD Thesis.

Montgomery, Chris. 2016. Perceptual prominence of city-based dialect areas in Great Britain. *Cityscapes and perceptual dialectology: Global perspectives on non-linguists' knowledge of the dialect landscape*, ed. by Jennifer Cramer and Chris Montgomery, 185–207. Berlin: Mouton de Gruyter.

Montgomery, Chris, and Phillip Stoeckle. 2013. Geographical information systems and perceptual dialectology. *Journal of Linguistic Geography* 1.52–85.

Montgomery, Chris, and Jennifer Cramer. 2016. Developing methods in perceptual dialectology. *Cityscapes and perceptual dialectology: Global perspectives on non-linguists' knowledge of the dialect landscape*, ed. by Jennifer Cramer and Chris Montgomery, 9–24. Berlin: Mouton de Gruyter.

Montgomery, Michael. 2008. The Southern accent—Alive and well. *Southern cultures: The fifteenth anniversary reader*, ed. by H. L. Watson and L. J. Griffin, 95–113. Chapel Hill, NC: University of North Carolina Press.

Niedzielski, Nancy, and Dennis R. Preston. 2020. Pholk phonetics and phonology. *Approaches to the study of sound structure and speech: Interdisciplinary work in honour of Katarzyna Dziubalska-Kołaczyk*, ed. by Magdalena Wrembel, Agnieszka Kiełkiewicz-Janowiak, and Piotr Gasiorowski, 87–108. New York: Routledge.

Oxley, Meghan. 2015. *Southern, Texan, or both? Southernness and identity in Deer Park, Texas*. Seattle, WA: University of Washington Ph.D. dissertation.

Preston, Dennis R. 1989. *Perceptual dialectology: Nonlinguists' views of areal linguistics*. Dordrecht, the Netherlands: Foris.

Preston, Dennis R. 1993. The uses of folk linguistics. *International Journal of Applied Linguistics* 3.181–259.

Preston, Dennis R. 1996. Where the worst English is spoken. *Varieties of English around the world: Focus on the USA*, ed. by E. Schneider, 297–360. Amsterdam: John Benjamins.

Preston, Dennis R. (ed.) 1999. *Handbook of perceptual dialectology*, vol. 1. Amsterdam: John Benjamins.

Preston, Dennis R. 2002. Language with an attitude. *The handbook of language variation and change*, ed. by J.K. Chambers, P. Trudgill, and N. Shilling-Estes, 40–66. Malden, MA: Wiley-Blackwell.

Preston, Dennis R. 2010. Variation in language regard. *Variatio delectat: Empirische Evidenzen und theoretische Passungen sprachlicher Variation* (für Klaus J. Mattheier zum 65. Geburtstag), ed. by E. Zeigler, P. Gilles, & J. Scharloth, 7–27. Frankfurt: Peter Lang.

Preston, Dennis R. 2018. Language regard: What, why, how, whither. *Language regard: Methods, variation and change*, ed. by B.E. Evans, E.J. Benson, and J.N. Stanford, 3–28. Cambridge: Cambridge University Press.

Rensink, W.G. 1955. Informant classification of dialects. Reprinted in D. Preston (1999), 3–7.

Rodgers, Elena. 2016. A rhetorical analysis of folk linguistic discourse: The case of twang. *American Speech* 91.393–424.

Ryan, Ellen B., and Howard Giles (eds.) 1982. *Attitudes towards language variation*. London: Edward Arnold.

Sibata, Takesi. 1959. Consciousness of dialect boundaries. Reprinted in D. Preston (1999), 39–62.

Tamasi, Susan. 2003. *Cognitive patterns of linguistic perceptions*. Athens, GA: University of Georgia dissertation.

Weijnen, Antonius A. 1946. De grenzen tussen de Oost-Noordbrabantse dialecten onderling [The borders between the dialects of eastern North Brabant]. *Oost-Noordbrabantse dialectproblemen [Eastern North Brabant dialect problems]*, ed. by A.A. Weijnen, J.M. Renders, and J. van Ginneken. Bijdragen en Mededelingen der Dialectencommissie van de Koninklijke Nederlandse Akademie van Wetenschappen te Amsterdam 8.1–15.

3

EXPLORING PLANET USA

Introduction

As an example of the application of the linguistic planets of belief metaphor, we spend this chapter exploring the ideas respondents have about the speakers and language varieties spoken in the US as a whole. We set the stage with a discussion of why the scale and size of maps matter, which will provide the foundation for understanding the variation in perceptions that exist as we zoom into regional and local levels in the following chapters. When we look at maps on different scales, for example, a map of the US, a map of the state of Tennessee, or a map of Nashville, Tennessee, we won't see the same perceptions neatly translated from one level to another. On the national map, for instance, Tennessee might be represented as part of the South, but after zooming in, there will be parts of the state that are more or less Southern; then, when we move to the town level, the idea of Southernness might not even be explicitly addressed by respondents. In fact, the same person can create significantly different maps, depending on the level of scale that is being represented. How does this happen? How do we maintain all of these different mental maps, while holding strong opinions about all of the various regions?

In this chapter, we draw on our own data as well as other perceptual dialectology studies to describe the linguistic planets of belief. Our respondents were given US maps so they could present their ideas about varieties spoken throughout the country. Results suggest that, when asked for national-level perceptions, respondents leave vast regions uncounted for in their descriptions, those regions that are labeled tend to rely heavily on superficial stereotypes, and even the home regions of the respondents rarely go beyond a combination of well-known caricatures of the people living there. We will explore the importance of geography, culture, history, social networks (Milroy 1987), and more in understanding how nonlinguists approach the task of dividing up the dialect landscape of the United States as a whole.

Scalability of maps and perceptions

In Chapter 2 we introduced different ways that maps are used as tools in perceptual dialectology to elicit linguistic perceptions from nonlinguists. As mentioned, the size of the area depicted on the maps used in these tasks mattered to participants because the size itself seemed to serve as an anchor for various types of beliefs, including ones that changed with differently sized maps. And in cases when maps didn't include the geographical regions they wanted to comment on, respondents often found a way to add what they considered important in the white space around the maps. One of the reasons why maps are used as a tool in perceptual dialectology is because of the functionality of maps in our daily lives. In other words, in American society we use the concept of a map, both literally and metaphorically, in how we talk about space and how we process the world around us, and therefore, in perceptual dialectology we can use it to elicit and reference ideas about the world. However, we do not suppose that there is a one-to-one correspondence between cognitive maps and geographic maps; as Downs and Stea (2011:313) assert: 'Above all, we should avoid getting locked into a form of thinking through which we as investigators force a subject to produce a cartographic cognitive map and which we then verify against an "objective" cartographic map'. With such an understanding of the relation between cartographic and cognitive maps, in this chapter we focus on the mental maps we create to understand the world, and then we use physical maps of the US to show how our mental maps and beliefs may be anchored and shaped by our understanding of this world.

We orient ourselves to both the physical world and our perception of its representation on maps. We use maps to determine how to travel from one place to another, we create maps of places in our minds to orient ourselves, and we refer to distances and places on those mental or physical maps that we then share with others (Downs & Stea 2011:312). The findings in the field of cognitive mapping show the intrinsic role that maps play in our lives, to the extent that 'we are concerned with phenomena so much part of our everyday lives and normal behavior that we naturally overlook them and take them for granted' (Downs & Stea 2011:312). For example, as we regularly rely on technologies like GPS navigation and Google Maps, the process of map creation and its influence on how we think about our surroundings may elude us. However, in moments of being physically lost and without technology to rely on, we might explicitly think about our spatial perceptions and how they are based on our own experiences with the world. Our cognitive maps are built throughout life and are accompanied by countless impressions and beliefs we have about our physical surroundings, the scale of these surroundings, and the people who inhabit them. Although it would make an easy visual metaphor to think about our mental maps on different scales mimicking the way we zoom in and out on Google Earth, the various levels are not the same. The roadmap of this part of our planet of belief is more complicated than that.

With regard to language, when we construct mental maps of speech patterns, proximity (e.g. Montgomery 2012) between speakers (whether physical or social) plays an important role. We speak mostly to others who are close to us, geographically and socially. Therefore, proximity has to be taken into account when considering what we think about the speech and speakers around us. We know more about our local communities, and we have more dense and multiplex interactions (e.g. Milroy 1987; Kretzschmar 2009) with people who share the same locale as us. Milroy (1987) described social networks of people as being the structure of a speech community. The web of individuals created within a community by various kinds of contact builds out an entire structure within which we can understand the spread, distribution, and diffusion of various linguistic structures. This structure can be described by metrics like density (more network connections means denser networks) and multiplexity (the different ways in which two actors might be connected; for example, two people may be related by a father–son relationship and a pastor–congregant one).

The more distance, geographic and social, there is between speakers, the less common the linguistic experiences and information they have. Through distance, linguistic variation creeps in, leading to differences even in communities in close geographical proximity to each other. For example, the speech of Knoxville, Tennessee, is different in some respects from the speech of Nashville, Tennessee, despite the two cities being only about a 2.5-hour drive from one another. Therefore, we want to think of proximity as a gradual process as we experience the world. We make connections between people and localities as we experience them indirectly and directly. The process of creating the various representations of localities on different scales is not easily predictable or explainable. But, here the tools of perceptual dialectology come into play, as they can help elicit ideas respondents have about other speakers and the varieties they use. As Downs and Stea (2011:314) point out: 'Some aspects of our composite cognitive maps may resemble a cartographic map; others will depend upon linguistic signatures (in which scale and rotation operations are irrelevant), and still others upon visual imagery signatures derived from eye-level viewpoints (in which the scale transformation may be disjointed or convoluted)'. Therefore, the process of eliciting beliefs anchored in locations becomes a complicated endeavor. This is why the metaphor of planets of belief is a useful visual tool that refers to familiar realities and is connected to cognitive maps, but at the same time it does not require or expect a one-to-one correspondence to a cartographic map of the world.

One possible explanation for the differences in scale between various composite cognitive maps can be found in a linguistic approach called LINGUISTICS OF SPEECH. Linguistics of speech proposes treating speech as a complex system that has 'a property of scaling, or nesting' (Kretzschmar 2009:179). Using this approach, we can see patterns in language by plotting frequencies of words. These frequencies follow the pattern of an asymptotic curve, or A-curve, in which only a fraction of words in any given body of text (spoken or written) occur with the highest frequency (function words and the most prominent content words) and the rest of the words fall into the middle curve and the long tail of single-digit occurrences (Figure 3.1). The shape of the curve does not change when we zoom into or out of the data: only the linguistic details change. Because of this, predictions from one level to another (state to country, for example) will fail, since the most frequent descriptions will differ at each of these levels. For example, when we gathered the labels placed on a national map of the US by 180 respondents (a study discussed below in detail) and plotted the frequencies of content words in the labels, we found words like 'accent', 'Southern', and 'Northern' to be the most frequent ones (Figure 3.1). Such a distribution shows, for example, that respondents from Tennessee mostly commented on people's accents and focused on the divisions between North and South.

As shown in Figure 3.1, a few words have high frequency, and then there is a sudden dip in occurrences, followed by a long tail of ONCERS. Such a distribution, an A-curve, is found throughout language data. Because of the scalability feature of language, as proposed by linguistics of speech, we observe A-curves throughout all the composite result maps. However, we cannot take one of the A-curves, such as the one presented as Figure 3.1, and predict what the distribution of the words will be at a different scale. This is exemplified by the following A-curves from the same data set. Figure 3.2 shows the distribution of labels assigned to the Northern region under the category Yankee, and Figure 3.3 shows the distribution of labels assigned to the West Coast, specifically to the California area.

Firstly, by merely looking at the distribution in Figure 3.1, we would not be able to predict the distributions in Figures 3.2 and 3.3. We should expect the same

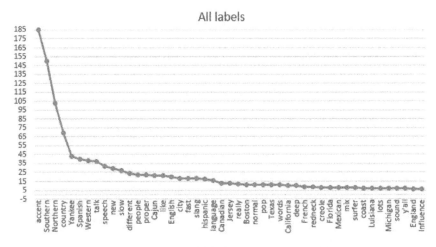

FIGURE 3.1 A-curve distribution of all labels from 180 maps of the US.

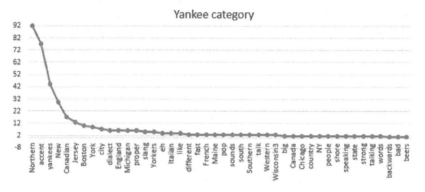

FIGURE 3.2 A-curve distribution of labels assigned to the Yankee category.

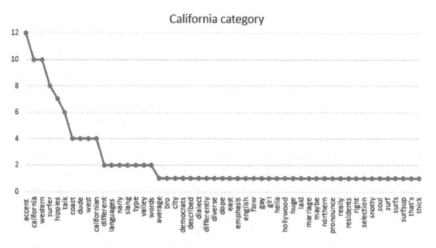

FIGURE 3.3 A-curve distribution of labels assigned to the California category.

shape – an A-curve – but not where the words fall in these distributions. When we zoom in from the national-level scale of all labels (Figure 3.1) to the regional view (Figure 3.2), we can see that the label 'Northern' is now in the top spot and 'Southern' ranks among the oncers. In the California region (Figure 3.2), 'Northern' is a oncer, 'Southern' has disappeared altogether, and words that were in the tail of the distribution at the national-level scale are now at the top. Through this illustration, we can see that the scale of the map used in data collection matters. The different scales of the map showing various sizes of geographical areas reveal different views of the results. If we follow the approach proposed by linguistics of speech, we cannot predict the results of one scale to another.

Moreover, research conducted by the Horvaths in Australia and New Zealand illustrates differences in scales. This work has 'demonstrated the idea of what they call "scale dependency" in speech by pointing out that the variation in speech looks different depending on how the observer groups the data' (Kretzschmar 2009:237). Focusing on /l/ vocalization in Australia and New Zealand, Horvath and Horvath (2003) studied 312 speakers from nine localities. Their data shows that the percentages of /l/ vocalization at various levels of aggregation did not correspond to each other. In other words, the percentage established for the regional level was not found at the national or local levels. It is simply impossible to predict performance at higher levels from lower levels, or vice versa. As Kretzschmar explains, although the Horvaths didn't present their data as A-curves, the scale dependency can be observed when we look at the results on different scales of regionality. As Table 3.1 shows, the vocalization has a different distribution at the local, regional, national, and supranational levels. According to the researchers, 'place consistently made the most important contribution to the variability of /l/ vocalization for all three supranational analyses' (Horvath & Horvath 2003:166). However, if the frequencies for all of the various levels were graphed, they all would have the shape of an A-curve, with the only difference being the ranking of specific variants. Some variants would have a higher or lower rank from level to level, and some would not appear at all on particular levels. Therefore, since there is no one-to-one correspondence between features at various levels, we are not able to predict the behavior of a group of speakers from the behaviors of individual speakers, or vice versa.

TABLE 3.1 Rates of /l/ vocalization (adapted from Table 2, Horvath & Horvath 2003:147)

Geographical scale	Rate of /l/ vocalizations
Supranational	
• Australasian	33%
National	
• Australia	15%
• New Zealand	58%
Regional	
• SE Queensland	3%
• SE Australia	11%
• S Australia	28%
• New Zealand	58%
Local	
• Brisbane	3%
• Melbourne	9%
• Sydney	15%
• Hobart	10%
• Mt. Gambier	28%
• Adelaide	26%
• Auckland	57%
• Wellington	58%
• Christchurch	60%

The scalability proposed in linguistics of speech applies not only to produced speech, but also to collected perceptions of speech. The varying rankings of perceptions on A-curves were visible in research conducted on perceptions of space on local and national levels by Gould and White (1986). They established that there were differences in the perceptions of local surroundings between speakers from the same neighborhood, based on research done by Ladd (1967), in which children from a neighborhood in Boston were asked to draw a map of their locale. Depending on the type of feature that was most important to them, the children emphasized different factors, such as their immediate surroundings or the ethnic divisions of the neighborhood. Therefore, the maps were substantially different from one another. In addition, Gould and White (1986) solicited perceptions of the most desirable places to live in North America and Britain. It turned out that, on one hand, the national perceptual representations were different from one another, as they carried the 'local domes' of preference (where the concept of 'domes' represented local areas as most desirable); on the other hand, except for those 'local domes', the national preferences were very similar. 'Thus, it is possible and useful to talk about national preferences, at the same time that "local domes" consistently appear in the data, and at the same time that we know that individual spatial perceptions are likely to be very different from each other' (Kretzschmar 2009:227). In all of the research presented, we find time after time that no individual's map matches the national map exactly, and from no national map were we able to predict the shape of an individual's map.

So far, the word *map* has been used for two different concepts in linguistic research presented in this book. The first concept is as a data collection tool, where informants are given physical maps to use as anchors on which to place their beliefs in the form of labels for speech, people, regions, and stereotypes. These cartographic maps can be produced to represent various levels of scale, starting from the national level, to regional, state, or single-town or neighborhood levels. Along these lines, we also use them as the underlayer for composite result maps to showcase the aggregated compilation of respondents' maps. The second way to use this concept is with cognitive maps, in which,

> the individual receives information from a complex, uncertain, changing and unpredictable source via a series of imperfect sensory modalities, operating over varying time spans and intervals between time spans. From such diversity the individual must aggregate information to form a comprehensive representation of the environment. This process of acquisition, amalgamation and storage is cognitive mapping, and the product of this process at any point of time can be considered a cognitive map.
>
> (Downs & Stea 2011:313)

As expected, such a process of acquisition is complex and idiosyncratic, producing a great deal of variation in how each person perceives the world. Therefore, perceptual dialectology research attempts to capture this relationship between cartographic and cognitive maps, while at the same time fully recognizing

> that a cognitive map is not necessarily a 'map'. […] We are using the term 'map' to designate a functional analogue. The focus of attention is on a cognitive representation which has the functions of the familiar cartographic map but not necessarily the physical properties of such a pictorial graphic model (Blaut et al. 1970). […] The carto-graphic map has a profound effect on our concept of a cognitive map.
>
> (Downs & Stea 2011:313)

Therefore, the metaphorical connection between the two concepts creates complexities and nuances that we can begin to investigate with the use of cartographic maps to elicit cognitive maps and explain through the planets of belief metaphor.

National-level maps

The differences between speakers and their perceptions of speech can be clearly seen in the research performed by Preston (1989), introduced in Chapter 2. He used the 'Draw-a-map' methodology, with maps filled in by respondents from Hawaii, Michigan, southern Indiana, western New York, and New York City. The respondents were asked to draw areas of regional speech on the map and label them. The five visions of America given by these different groups provide many differences in the way they specifically demarcate the boundaries between varieties of speech they see being different from their own.

The composite maps showcasing the visions of America by these five groups are presented in Figures 3.4 through 3.8.

The size and concrete geographical location of areas such as the Southern dialect varied due to maps including different states or parts of states; for example, Texas is included in the South for the Hawaiian respondents, but not for the other respondents. Moreover, the West seems to be the most variable space indicated on the maps. All groups used it differently: Hawaiians didn't indicate it at all,

> the Michigan respondents see West as the territory just west of them; the Indiana respondents use it as a coastal term, and both groups of New York respondents use it as a large cover term for areas geographically west in general.
>
> (Preston 1989:120)

Nevertheless, across all five visions of America some similar regions also appear. For instance, no one forgot to put the South or North on the maps, and Midwest was a commonly recognized area. Such commonalities may be showcasing shared ideas in the planets of belief of the respondents. If we look at Table 3.2,

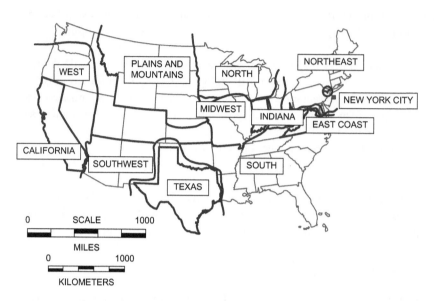

FIGURE 3.4   Composite of hand-drawn maps of regional dialects from the point of view of southern Indiana respondents. Source: Courtesy of Preston (1989:114).

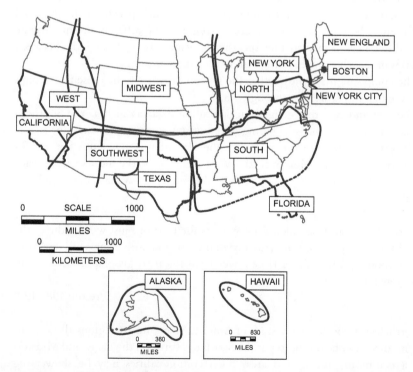

FIGURE 3.5   Composite of hand-drawn maps of regional dialects from the point of view of New York City respondents. Source: Courtesy of Preston (1989:114).

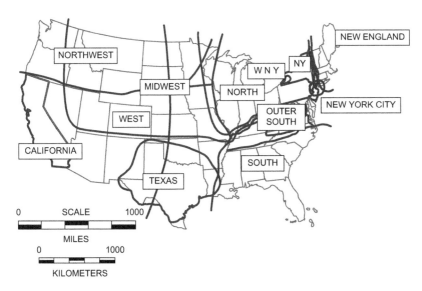

FIGURE 3.6 Composite of hand-drawn maps of regional dialects from the point of view of New York respondents. Source: Courtesy of Preston (1989:115).

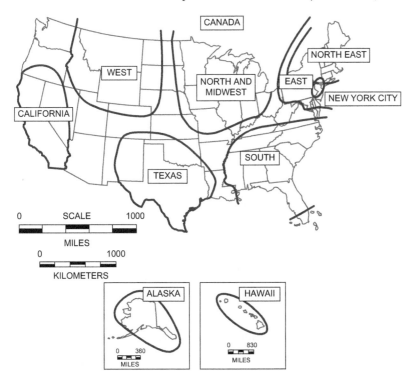

FIGURE 3.7 Composite of hand-drawn maps of regional dialects from the point of view of southeastern Michigan respondents. Source: Courtesy of Preston (1989:116).

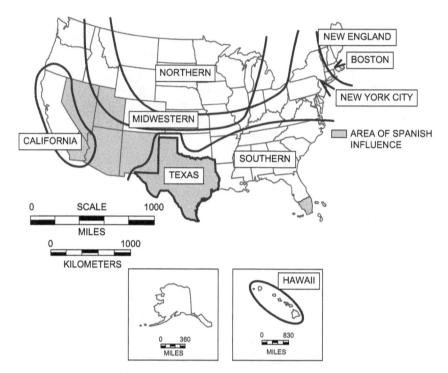

FIGURE 3.8   Composite of hand-drawn maps of regional dialects from the point of view of Hawaiian respondents. Source: Courtesy of Preston (1989:116).

which points out specific states and regions, and their frequency in appearing on respondent maps, we notice patterns of more salient regions that may reveal the ways in which their belief planets are also quite similar.

Table 3.2 reveals some interesting patterns. Firstly, the South is indicated by almost all respondents no matter where they reside. The higher the percentage in the parentheses, the more informants indicated some sort of perceptual region in that geographical location. Therefore, the South is the most prominent area that is indicated (.94), followed by the Midwest (.55), New York City (.44), and Texas (.43). Such a pattern is not surprising if we consider one of Preston's (1989) main observations about his data: those places where linguistic and cultural caricatures are attached show up as most prominent in the results. This suggests, in our model, that the belief planets are most stable for these patterns. Preston indicated that this notion oftentimes appears together with large areas unaccounted for by any of the speakers. 'This space suggests that respondents have no experience with an area, that an area has no characteristic linguistic features or stereotypes, or that an area has no popular cultural notoriety' (1989:121). In other words, what the map task seems to elicit is ideas that are very prominent

TABLE 3.2 Identification and intensity of identification of US speech areas by young, White (and Asian, Hawaii only), well-educated residents of Hawaii, southern Indiana, western New York, southeastern Michigan, and New York City

	HAW N = 35	SI N = 35	WNY N = 22	SEM N = 21	NYC N = 25	Total N = 138
Alaska	–	–	–	7 (.33)	5 (.20)	12 (.08)
Boston	9 (.26)	–	–	–	7 (.28)	16 (.12)
California	11 (.31)	11 (.31)	5 (.23)	20 (.95)	8 (.32)	55 (.40)
Canada	–	–	–	6 (.29)	–	6 (.04)
East	–	–	–	9 (.43)	–	9 (.07)
East Coast	–	6 (.17)	–	–	–	6 (.04)
Florida	–	–	–	–	5 (.20)	5 (.04)
Hawaii	34 (.97)	–	–	8 (.38)	8 (.32)	50 (.36
Indiana	–	5 (.14)	–	–	–	5 (.04)
Midwest	22 (.63)	12 (.34)	8 (.36)	13 (.62)*	21 (.84)	76 (.55)
New England	6 (.17)	–	14 (.64)	–	16 (.64)	36 (.26)
New York	–	–	5 (.23)	–	8 (.32)	13 (.09)
NY City	20 (.57)	5 (.14)	10 (.45)	10 (.48)	16 (.64)	61 (.44)
North	8 (.23)	13 (.37)	6 (.27)	13 (.62)*	6 (.24)	46 (.33)
Northeast	–	24 (.69)	–	7 (.33)	–	31 (.22)
Northwest	–	–	7 (.32)	–	–	7 (.05)
Plains and Mountains	–	8 (.23)	–	–	–	8 (.06)
South	33 (.94)	31 (.89)	22 (1.00)	21 (1.00)	23 (.92)	130 (.94)
Southwest	–	8 (.23)	–	–	6 (.24)	14 (.10)
Spanish	12 (.34)	–	–	–	–	12 (.09)
Texas	13 (.37)	18 (.51)	10 (.45)	10 (.48)	8 (.32)	59 (.43)
Upper South	–	–	7 (.32)	–	–	7 (.05)
West	–	8 (.23)	14 (.56)	12 (.57)	14 (.56)	48 (.35)
West New York	–	–	5 (.23)	–	–	5 (.04)

Source: Courtesy of Preston (1989:117).

in our planets of belief or expose the gaps that we have about varieties spoken outside of our locale.

In the second part of the task, the respondents were asked to rate the speech of individual states with respect to two features, 'correct' and 'pleasant'. With regards to rankings of correctness, the South is marked as being the least correct and areas in the North and West as being most correct, as shown in Figure 3.9. The higher the number in the legend, the more incorrect the indicated area was perceived as being.

Figure 3.9 shows a cultural schema present in the planets of belief held by participants in Indiana. The states indicated as being least correct are located in the South, which, as Preston and others (e.g. Preston 1989; Preston 1996; Niedzielski & Preston 2000; Cramer 2016) have repeatedly shown, is the most perceptually salient region and an anchor for a multitude of stereotypes. Therefore, the South

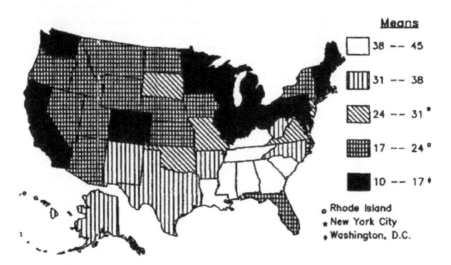

FIGURE 3.9 Regional perception of correct English by young, White, college-enrolled southern Indiana respondents. Source: Courtesy of Preston (1989:54).

is perceived as THE location for dialect, and one that is considered the most different from perceived standard or correct usage. On the other end of the spectrum, for these respondents, the most correct speech is connected to the areas that the residents are from, as well as close neighboring states.

But what happens if we ask about pleasantness of speech varieties? Preston tests the idea that originated in social psychology (e.g. Lambert et al. 1960; Bradac & Wisegarver 1984) that traits associated with language perceptions tend to fall into one of two categories, status or solidarity, using 'correctness' ratings as a stand-in for status and 'pleasantness' for solidarity. Figure 3.10 shows the results of the rankings given by respondents in Indiana; the lower the mean, the more pleasant the speech variety was ranked.

Indiana residents think that their variety is not only the most correct, but also the most pleasant (Figure 3.10). As Preston (1989:73) describes:

> California, Colorado, and Florida stand out on both pleasant and correct maps, and what is seen as a preference only for Maine in the pleasant task is extended to all of New England in the correct format. Washington is not distinct in the pleasant ratings (as it was for correct). The poorly-ranked Mississippi of the pleasant task is joined by Louisiana, Tennessee, Kentucky, Alabama, Georgia, and South Carolina in the correct map – making it a clear trend for those respondents to give low rankings to the South on both tasks.

Although the data clearly show that the negative beliefs about the South are present for the Indiana respondents, Preston shows that the results are not

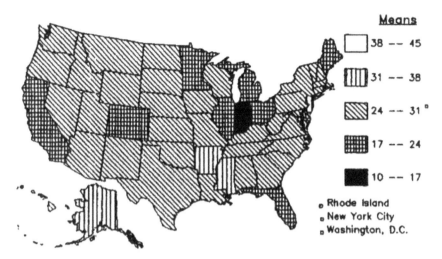

Means

☐ 38 -- 45

▥ 31 -- 38

▧ 24 -- 31 °

▦ 17 -- 24

■ 10 -- 17

▫ Rhode Island
▫ New York City
▫ Washington, D.C.

FIGURE 3.10   Pleasant English mean scores for the 50 states, New York City, and Washington, D.C., as ranked by young, White, well-educated southern Indiana residents. Source: Courtesy of Preston (1989:73).

representative beyond the scope of the sample, noting that if the respondents were from one of those poorly ranked states, at least the pleasantness ranking may look different. In fact, Preston included a map of pleasantness ranking done by Alabama respondents, and it shows a different view of the South, as seen in Figure 3.11.

The image of pleasant speech in the US looks different when shown from the perspective of Southern respondents (Figure 3.11). Alabamians think that the South is the place where pleasant speech is spoken. Following the assertions by Gould and White (1986) about local domes of preference, we should not be surprised that residents of a state think of their own speech as the most pleasant. However, the different visions of America appearing in Preston's (1989) work show that the cultural beliefs about the country may not be shared widely. What this indicates is that we care and know more about our immediate surroundings, and the further from us other speakers are, the more we have to fill in gaps in our ideas about them and rely on common stereotypes.

With regard to the planets of belief metaphor, the distance between particles can reflect the physical distance between the individual and different speech communities, leading one to have different ideas attached to speech that is closer vs. farther away. This notion gets even more complex and nuanced if we take into an account the distinction between the geographic and cognitive maps as described above. Our geographic maps are continuous and neat; our cognitive maps may be considered 'distorted' in comparison to them. The physical distance on a typical geography map might be larger or smaller than in our cognitive map. As explained in Downs and Stea (2011), and discussed above, when we create our

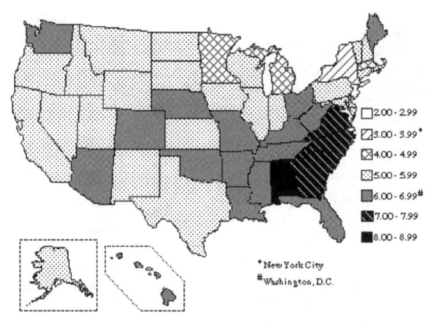

FIGURE 3.11 The 50 states, New York City, and Washington, D.C., rated for language pleasantness (1 = least pleasant, 10 = most pleasant) by Southern (chiefly Alabama) respondents (results are shaded by mean score ranges). Source: Courtesy of Preston (2015).

cognitive maps, we include various impressions of the world: geographic, social, historical, cultural. Using a geographic map to capture the cognitive maps we hold showcases many discrepancies between them.

To make this image even more complex we can compare the results above with a study of 68 respondents (60 of whom were Kentucky residents) in which we asked about their ideas of pleasantness and correctness in other states. Table 3.3 shows the states placed at the ends of the spectrum on the ratings of correctness, pleasantness, and similarity to Kentuckian speech (Cramer 2016).

TABLE 3.3 Comparisons of Kentucky speech to other states (Cramer 2016)

In comparison to Kentucky speech	State(s)
Most similar	Indiana, Kentucky
Most different	Louisiana
Least correct	Louisiana
Most correct	Washington D.C.
Least pleasant	New Jersey
Most pleasant	Kentucky

What these results show is that Kentuckians see the neighboring state of Indiana as being the most similar to them; speakers of Louisiana varieties, on the other hand, were not only seen as being the most different but also the least correct. And although Kentucky was not rated as the most correct variety (Washington, D.C., took that spot), it was considered the most pleasant. New Jersey speakers were the least pleasant to listen to, which is not surprising, as New Jersey and New York City areas are traditionally portrayed and perceived as being places with the least correct way of speaking (e.g. Preston 1996). When we look at larger regions, we see a similar trend. Table 3.4 showcases the ranking of regions by correctness and pleasantness.

If we look at the data on a different scale, here we see a vision of America that is slightly different. Just as we have discussed, the scale that we look at makes a difference in how we see the results aggregated. So, when we look at the state-level preferences in Table 3.4, we find that Kentuckians see themselves as being the most pleasant, but when we look at the South region including Kentucky, it does not float to the top of the pleasantness ranking: the Western region does. In other words, Kentucky might sound very pleasant to its speakers, but other states in the South do not rank as highly in this regard. We can see this also in the fact that Louisiana, a Southern state, was ranked as the least correct state, but at the regional level, it is the South including Kentucky that ranks lowest. Therefore, we see that different scales of our perceptions produce different results and looking at one level is not a good predictor of another level.

Now that it has been shown that perspective and scale matters, we can focus on a particular viewpoint from respondents who live in a part of the South that rarely needs to consider its own status as Southern: Tennessee. The Kentucky situation is complicated by being a border state for the South, but Tennessee is usually considered as having a solid footing in the South, with no issues of

TABLE 3.4 Correctness and pleasantness ranking by region for Kentucky respondents (Cramer 2016)

Region	Category	Ranking from most correct to least correct
Midland	Correct	1
West	Correct	2
Upper North	Correct	3
Other	Correct	4
South	Correct	5
South-KY	Correct	6
		Ranking from most pleasant to least pleasant
West	Pleasant	1
Other	Pleasant	2
South	Pleasant	3
South-KY	Pleasant	4
Midland	Pleasant	5
Upper North	Pleasant	6

having any kind of border status. However, as we will see in the sections below, just because the informants live in what others might consider to be unquestionably Southern, the vision of the America they have is far from simple and straightforward.

Planet USA according to Tennessee informants

To showcase an image of the US by a group of Southerners from Tennessee, Bounds and Sutherland (2018) conducted a study to gain insight into the beliefs held by these respondents. The study was based on 180 college students who were asked to fill in maps with their perceptions. The respondents' paper maps were scanned, georeferenced, and digitized using a heads-up technique in ArcMap (Bounds & Sutherland 2018). The digitization process involved tracing polygons that covered the areas of perceptions marked by the respondents (Figure 3.12). Each polygon was assigned with a text attribute from the text provided by the respondent on the map (Figure 3.13). Each respondent's map was then saved as a unique feature class in a geodatabase. This produces maps that showcase the distribution of various types of labels, in order to see not only where the perceptual boundaries were located, but also what type of label was attached to them. As presented in Figure 3.14, the way in which result maps are created allows for the showcasing of different levels of agreement, as displayed by the intensity of the color black. The darker the area, the more informants put something on the map.

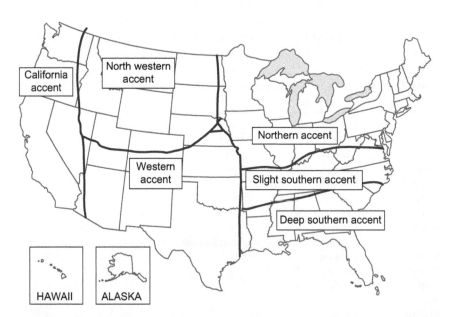

FIGURE 3.12 An informant's map with the US map layered underneath, ready to be georeferenced with polygons.

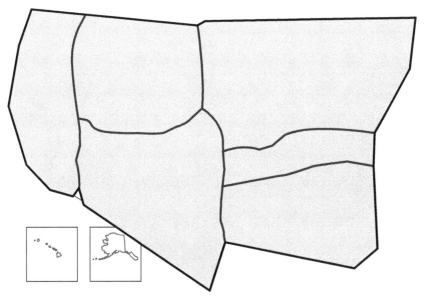

INF017NCA

OBJECTID	SHAPE	SHAPE_Length	SHAPE_Area	Filename	Label
1	Polygon	6637782.264424	2492974414931.4873	INF017NCA	western accent
2	Polygon	5386424.741628	1796090055551.9714	INF017NCA	deep southern accent
3	Polygon	4389550.383738	717985704159.02795	INF017NCA	slight southern accent
4	Polygon	5425590.43372	1405064169234.5298	INF017NCA	California accent
5	Polygon	7595876.988085	3203526454088.0996	INF017NCA	Northern accent
6	Polygon	5354199.023588	1963485523660.4185	INF017NCA	North Western accent

FIGURE 3.13   An informant's map with georeferenced polygons of their perception regions, plus labels attached to them, as referenced in the table.

The respondents drew areas on the maps and labeled them. When all labels from the national maps were entered, there was a total of 942 entries across 180 individual maps, averaging 4.8 labels per map. Seventy-nine areas indicated on individual maps were not given a label. Seventeen categories emerged from the data, listed in Table 3.5. We can clearly see that the Yankee/Southern distinction was the most highly noted by the respondents, followed by the linguistic description of the speech. Such a distribution of the labels once again points to the idea that we first indicate our home areas, then add in stereotypes and cultural schemas that are most prominent and often the most derogatory.

If we look at the distribution of these categories on the composite maps, we see that the label categories co-occur based on geographical location. We find labels associated with North (Linguistic Features, Yankee: a total of 314 labels), the

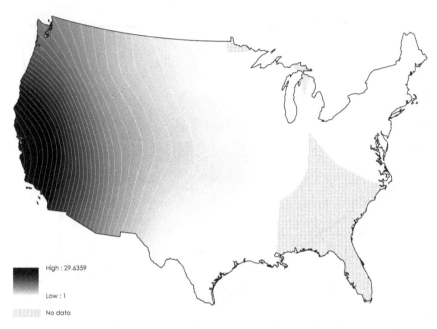

High : 29.6359

Low : 1

No data

FIGURE 3.14   Composite map from Tennessee respondents for all labels in the California category.

TABLE 3.5 Frequency of label categories

Label category	Frequency
Yankee	201
Southern	136
Linguistic features	113
No label	79
Spanish	71
Country	56
Miscellaneous	51
California	47
No accent	38
Cajun	36
South West	31
Uppity	24
Mixed	23
People	15
Mid-Western	10
Florida	7
AAVE	4

South (Southern, Country, Southwest, African American Vernacular English, Cajun, Florida: a total of 270 labels), West Coast (California, Mixed, No Label, Uppity, Spanish: a total of 244 labels), and North-West (People, Miscellaneous, No Accent: a total of 108 labels).

West Coast

From the description above, it seems that the Tennessee informants focused on four major regions of the US when labeling their perceptual regions. The two least frequent perceptual regions are located farther away from Tennessee than the two most frequently mentioned ones. This finding is not surprising: the more removed we are from any kind of speech, whether it is geographically, socially, and/or culturally, the less likely we are to know about it and its speakers, and the less likely we are to talk about them (e.g. Gould & White 1986; Tamasi 2003; Kretzschmar 2009). We begin the description of this particular vision of America from those areas farthest, geographically if not also socially or culturally, from the Tennessee respondents: the West Coast, followed by the Northeast. First, we turn to the labels that were associated with the West Coast region. It appears that the most distinguishing point for the West Coast for these Southern respondents was the state of California. Figures 3.14 and 3.15 show the results of the categories 'California' and 'Uppity', respectively.

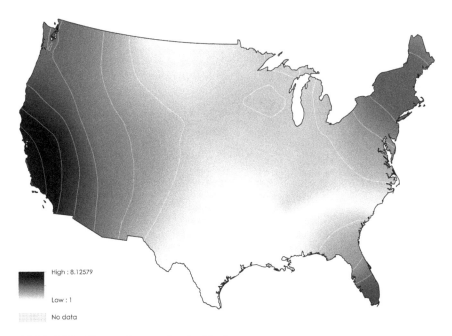

High : 8.12579

Low : 1

No data

FIGURE 3.15 Composite map for the Uppity category.

These two categories reveal an image of the beliefs about the West Coast from our Tennessee respondents. For one, the focus really is mostly on California, which is the epicenter of agreement on this issue. The West Coast is a vast geographical area, but what seems to be most recognizable to the informants is the part of the region that is probably the most propagated in mainstream media and the entertainment industry. The labels that were used to describe this region draw on the commonly known stereotypes of 'surfer dude', 'valley accent', or even more broadly 'California accent', as is seen in Figure 3.16. At the same time, as Table 3.6 shows, the Uppity category points to people living in these regions as 'proper rich people'. To add to this image, Figure 3.17 shows the distribution

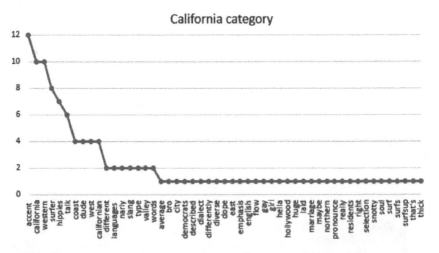

FIGURE 3.16 A-curve distribution of labels within the California category.

TABLE 3.6 Frequency of labels in the Uppity category

proper	7	fast	1
people	6	Florida	1
rich	6	kids	1
city	4	life	1
old	3	lost	1
talk	3	money	1
hip	2	preppy	1
ish	2	raspy	1
rude	2	retired	1
arrogant	1	slow	1
big	1	snobby	1
English	1	southerners	1
white	1	surfer	1
yippie	1	trendy	1
young	1	urban	1

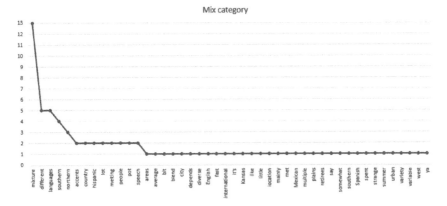

FIGURE 3.17 A-curve distribution of labels within the Mix category.

of labels in the Mix category (in which all labels point to some sort of mixing of people or speech, according to the respondents); we can see that California in the mind of the respondents is also a place of a lot of 'mixture' of 'different' 'languages' and 'accents'. Although the informants had varying ideas about the West Coast, a lot of them also didn't quite know how to label that region, as the result map shows. In Figure 3.18 we can see all the regions that were indicated on the map but were not labeled.

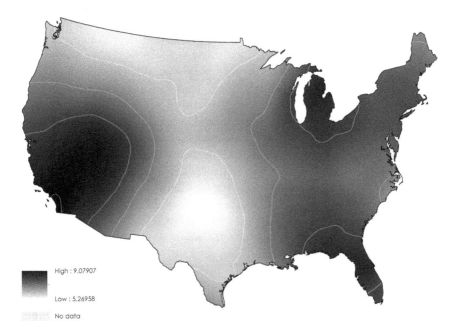

High : 9.07907

Low : 5.26958

No data

FIGURE 3.18 Composite map for the No Label category.

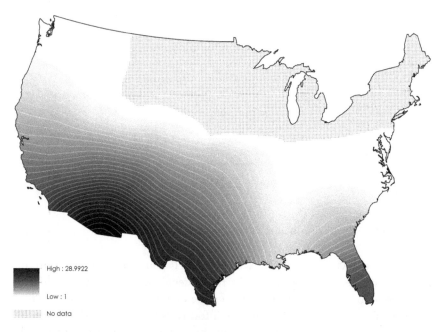

High : 28.9922

Low : 1

No data

FIGURE 3.19 Composite map for the Spanish category.

Finally, although this region was recognized for the diversity of languages and accents used there, Spanish was the language that was recognized most often on the maps. Figure 3.19 shows the distribution of this label.

The result map in Figure 3.19 shows that the epicenter for Spanish use, according to the informants, starts in Texas and stretches all the way to the West Coast, adding another layer of linguistic variety to this region. What labeling of the West Coast shows is that our sample of Tennesseans has a very surface knowledge of the region and its speech. The planet of belief concerned with the West Coast is built out of particles associated with and perpetuated by popular culture and the entertainment industry. The West Coast is closely associated with California, and the perceived network of speakers living there comprises surfers, rich people, various languages (with an emphasis on Spanish), and accents. The ideas about the West Coast held by the Tennesseans do not seem to have a heavy negative or positive attitude associated with them. Moreover, it appears that the planet of belief containing ideas about the West Coast shows that the informants bring in indirect experience with the region, such as media depictions of Californians, and does not represent a detailed network of direct encounters with speakers from the West Coast.

Northwest

The region that was the least described by the informants in the study was geographically the farthest one from Tennessee. The three categories of labels that

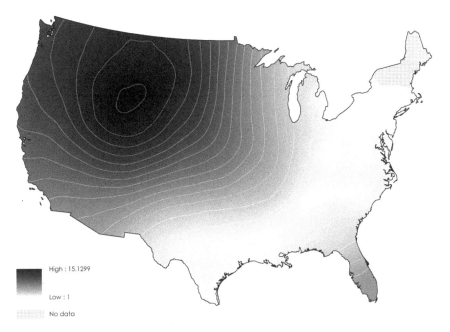

High : 15.1299

Low : 1

No data

FIGURE 3.20   Composite map for the Miscellaneous category.

were anchored in that area were those describing People, referring to a No Accent area, and falling into the category of Miscellaneous (a category of labels that didn't really fall into any other category). Figures 3.20 through 3.22 show the distribution of these results.

The distribution in the Miscellaneous and No Accent categories (Table 3.7) shows that the informants identify this region with a lack of accent, since the most frequently used labels were 'no accent' and 'normal English'. At the same time, however, there is a great deal of insecurity about the speech of that part of the country, since some of the most frequently used labels were 'Not Sure' and 'I don't know'. It could also be that the labels that the respondents do use are not easily categorized. From the 'normal English' and 'no accent' labels, it appears that there is a close connection with Standard English, which could explain why there isn't any further labeling – for respondents. The planet of belief about this region is scarce in detail, and the description points more to the lack of ideas rather than actual direct or indirect experiences with dialects in this region. The informants really just don't know; this vast region does not seem to be one of the planets of belief about their country.

As described in Chapter 2, informants may feel inclined to say something about all of the parts of the map given to them, even if they do not know much about them. Therefore, we see a relatively high rate of responses indicating lack of knowledge, rather than a complex image of speech and speakers in that region.

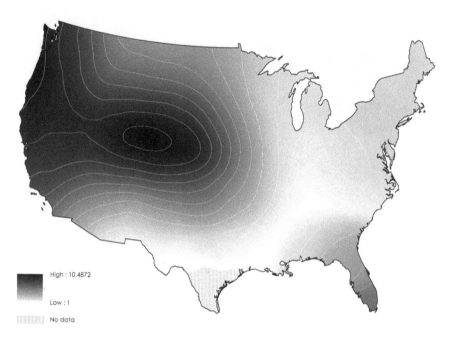

FIGURE 3.21 Composite map for the No Accent category.

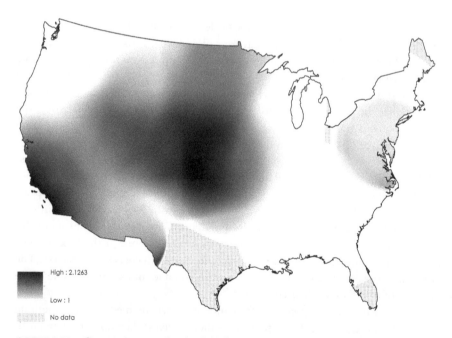

FIGURE 3.22 Composite map for the People category.

TABLE 3.7 Distribution of the top 10 most frequent labels in the Miscellaneous and No Accent categories

Misc		No accent	
know	7	accent	15
sure	5	normal	8
city	3	English	5
different	3	formal	4
Florida	2	people	3
idea	2	proper	3
like	2	standard	3
people	2	language	2
urban	2	plain	2
absolutely	1	speaking	2

This distribution points to a possible hole in the planet of belief for our group of Tennesseans. Downs and Stea (2011:315) explain such a relation between cartographic and cognitive maps in the following manner:

> The physical space of the real world is a continuous surface which we have come to understand through a classic geometrical framework: that of Euclid. […] There are no gaps or bottomless voids. […] Yet all cognitive maps are discontinuous surfaces. Seemingly some areas of the earth's surface do not exist when their existence is defined by the presence of phenomena in the subject's cognitive representation. […] [However] we must be careful in interpreting the absence of phenomena from cognitive maps as reflecting discontinuity of space.

In the sections above we saw that there are parts of the country where the informants didn't really provide greatly detailed descriptions of speech varieties. We speculate that this is probably closely connected to there being a large geographical distance between these places and a lack of direct experiences with the people who inhabit this region. Therefore, now we move on to the exploration of the region they are most familiar with: The South.

The South

The South, which is investigated as a separate planet of belief in Chapter 4, has the greatest variation in the number of categories that the Tennessee respondents associate with it. Altogether, there are 270 individual labels provided for the region, which makes it the second most labeled region in the US, indicating that the respondents had much to say about the South. Of course, this is to be expected since the respondents are native to the South, especially if we take into account that 'local identity is not strong unless the area has some linguistic or other caricature which helps promote such identification' (Preston 1989: 118). We can see that people who have the most experience with an area will likely have much to say about it, and thus, will have more depth and nuance within their planet of belief for that location. The composite maps presented in Figures 3.23–3.28 show the categories associated with the region geographically described as the South.

The areas covered by the labels in the Southern and Country categories are almost identical, which comes as no surprise since these words are often used interchangeably. The maps show that respondents see the areas of South Carolina, Georgia, Alabama, Mississippi, and Tennessee, as well as parts of Louisiana, Arkansas, and North Carolina, as the main, most agreed upon geographical portions of the South. This geographical area is the region that is shown repeatedly and most consistently in other perceptual studies. However, while there are some core states consistently indicated as being a part of the South, we also see that the precise boundaries are impossible to ascertain with much confidence. On Preston's maps (Figures 3.7 and 3.8), the boundaries are not the same for each group of respondents, and depending on what level of agreement is decided upon, the areas indicated can be extended or diminished significantly. The same is true for the Southern and Country categories. If we look at the areas indicated in the lighter shades of gray, the South expands to contain the area all the

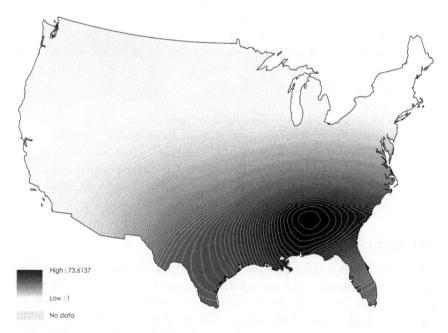

FIGURE 3.23 Composite map for the Southern category.

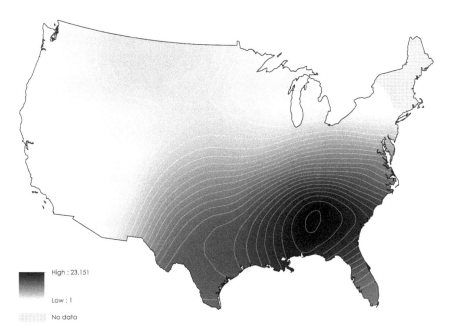

High : 23.151

Low : 1

No data

FIGURE 3.24 Composite map for the Country category.

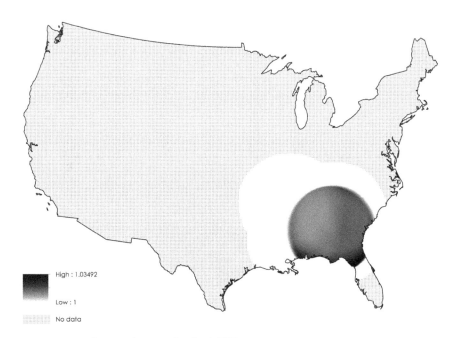

High : 1.03492

Low : 1

No data

FIGURE 3.25 Composite map for the AAVE category.

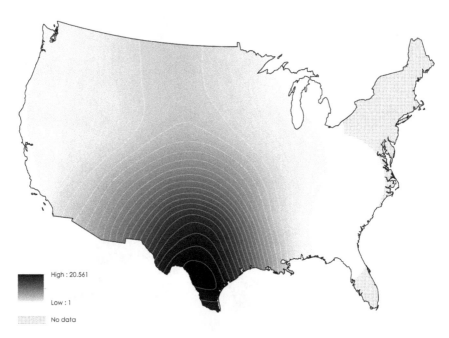

High : 20.561

Low : 1

No data

FIGURE 3.26 Composite map for the South West category.

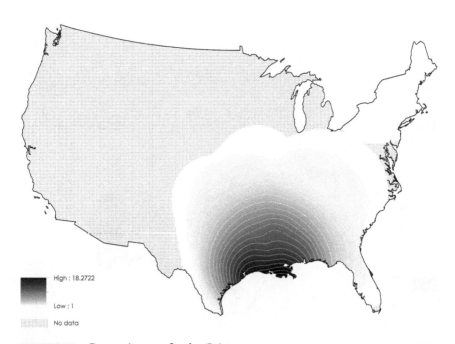

High : 18.2722

Low : 1

No data

FIGURE 3.27 Composite map for the Cajun category.

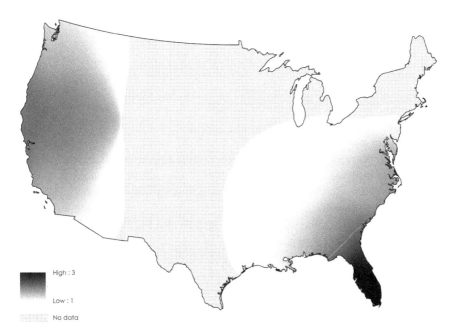

High : 3

Low : 1

No data

FIGURE 3.28   Composite map for the Florida category.

way to Texas in the West and Florida in the South. Therefore, we recognize Kretzschmar's (2009:231) assertion that: 'Preston's research clearly tells us that, even though just about all of his respondents named the South as a dialect region in some way, respondents could not agree where it was even in gross terms, not to mention detailed boundaries'.

Such a claim can be seen as the foundation of how we acknowledge variation in the way our planets of belief are constructed and structured. If all of our planets were constructed the same way, the maps would have precise and clean boundaries and all speakers would agree on where the South or the North is, but study after study tells a different story. The variation in the labels as described here shows that, on one hand, planets of belief have some commonalities that rely on stereotypes of the South, while on the other hand, the perception of the South is complex and nuanced, especially among residents of the South.

The remaining four categories of result maps in the South showcase four regions commonly included as part of the geographic South, but they are also unique in and of themselves.

These four regions are known for their unique speech that, although technically part of the South, also have their own characteristics that stand out. For example, many studies, including those already discussed in this chapter with respondents from Tennessee and Kentucky, consistently show that Florida is not included in the region of the South. In Tamasi (2003), Florida was one of five states (along with Alaska, California, Hawaii, and Texas) to be perceived by Georgia residents as standing on its own, separate from the geographic region to which it technically should belong. Moreover, Florida figures prominently in the Mix, Spanish, and No Accent categories as well. In this regard, respondents pointed to speakers there using mixed varieties (either mixed with Spanish or another English variety), while others indicated that people there did not have any accent. Florida is a good example of how respondent planets must juggle conflicting views.

When the informants described the Southern accent, they drew from well-known stereotypical ideas about Southerners. While these beliefs and stereotypes will be fully explored in Chapter 4, it is important to note that even if we look at the raw counts of the words used in the labels in this data, we see a certain image created by the respondents, as illustrated by the A-curve distributions in Figures 3.29 and 3.30 for the Southern category and Country category, respectively.

We might expect to get more complex answers here from people who reside in the region and find that there would be less reliance on common stereotypes. However, if we lemmatize the results for the Southern category (Table 3.8) and the Country category (Table 3.9), we find these to be the most common descriptions: Southerners have a Southern accent, they live in the South, and they are country. Even when we look at the labels that fall in the middle range of the frequency tables and the one-time labels in the tail, we see that the speakers don't have many detailed ideas about the region. However, the majority of respondents are from the South. So, the question remains, why wouldn't they be more specific and variable in their responses? It seems possible that, although residents of the region have more dense and multiplex experiences (e.g., Milroy 1987; Kretzschmar 2009) with their local perceptual region, this doesn't necessarily translate into more detail and complex descriptions of the region because of the scale of the cartographic map given. It is possible that on such a distant scale they

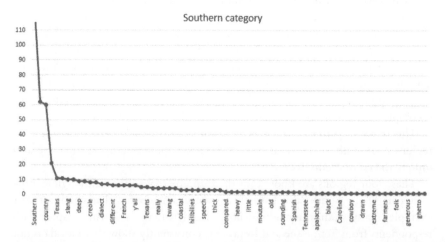

FIGURE 3.29 A-curve distribution of labels within the Southern category.

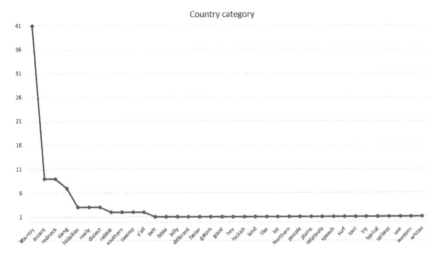

FIGURE 3.30   A-curve distribution of labels within the Country category.

rely on stereotypes and common caricatures to showcase what they think about their region.

For its residents, the South on these national-level maps does not appear very differently than how it does for respondents from other parts of the US. Although we might expect the Southerners to be more complex and nuanced in their description of their own region, results do not suggest that it is the case. The factor that may be at play here is scale. When we ask people to tell us what they think about speakers in the whole country, perhaps it is not that surprising that their descriptions are high-level generalizations that are handy, but not specific. Our planets of belief show, then, that as much as we may have detailed experiences with our surrounding areas, we may also have generalized ideas about the region, no matter how much or how little we have experienced it. These beliefs may be strongly connected to each other, which we see in terms appearing at the top of the A-curve, since those suggest that they form a tightly connected network of particles in the planets of belief.

The North

The Southern respondents seemed to draw from common ideas that are shared nationally to describe the South, but does having a shared view differ when they look at their heavily commented on but distant Northern neighbors? According to the respondents from Tennessee, the only thing to comment on is the fact that the North is where Yankees live. The two label categories that are geographically placed in the North are 'Yankee' and 'Linguistic Features' (labels in this category contain any type of commentary on speech and speech features or examples, such

TABLE 3.8 Lemmas for the South category

Southern	115	Florida	3
Accent	62	compared	2
Country	60	general	2
Cajun	21	heavy	2
Texas	11	little	2
Louisiana	11	Mex	2
Slang	10	mountain	2
Western	10	Northern	2
Deep	9	old	2
Talk	9	rabble	2
Creole	8	sounding	2
Redneck	8	southeast	2
Dialect	7	Spanish	2
Cowboy	7	swamp	2
Different	6	Tennessee	2
Slow	6	Alabama	1
French	6	Appalachian	1
Drawl	6	bit	1
y'all	6	black	1
States	5	bumpkin	1
Texans	5	Carolina	1
Ebonics	4	Coke	1
Really	4	cowboy	1
Rednecks	4	depending	1
Twang	4	drawn	1
Speak	4	excluding	1
Coastal	3	extreme	1
English	3	far	1
Hillbillies	3	farmers	1
People	3	fashioned	1
Speech	3	folk	1
State	3	generic	1
Thick	3	generous	1
		Georgia	1
		ghetto	1
		howdy	1

as talking fast, using a New York accent, and slang). Their distributions on result maps are presented in Figures 3.31 and 3.32.

The most frequent category was Yankee. On the surface it may be surprising that the Southerners (all participants were from Tennessee) pointed out their Northern 'nemesis' most frequently, but if we take into account that these maps allow informants to indicate their own stereotypes about people who are different from them, it may not be so surprising that the Southerners were ready to say something about the 'damn Yankees'. As shown in Figure 3.31, the area where the highest level of agreement occurs is New England. But unlike

TABLE 3.9 Lemmas for the Country category

Country	41	gators	1
Accent	9	good	1
Redneck	9	hey	1
Slang	7	hickish	1
Hillbillies	3	kind	1
Really	3	like	1
Dialect	3	lot	1
Rabble	2	Northern	1
Southern	2	people	1
Swamp	2	plains	1
y'all	2	relatively	1
Belt	1	speech	1
Bible	1	surf	1
Billy	1	tool	1
Different	1	try	1
Faster	1	typical	1
Gators	1	upbeat	1
Whites	1	use	1
		western	1

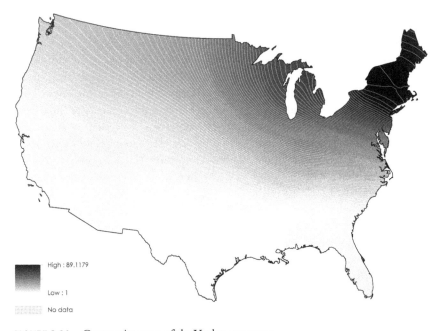

High : 89.1179

Low : 1

No data

FIGURE 3.31 Composite map of the Yankee category.

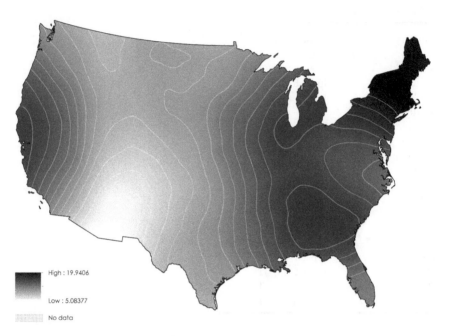

High : 19.9406

Low : 5.08377

No data

FIGURE 3.32   Composite map of Linguistic Features category.

other composite maps, Figure 3.32 shows that almost the entire country could be categorized as Yankee. Indeed, at least one person drawing an individual map enclosed some portion of the entire country except for small portions of Texas, Arizona, New Mexico, and Florida within the Yankee category. That type of distribution once again points to the A-curve distribution of the labels: we have a high number of respondents agreeing on a low number of areas, and a high number of areas are only indicated by one informant apiece. Therefore, on a very low level of agreement, we see almost all of the country indicated as being part of this category, and at the highest level of agreement, we find a relatively small area.

In the geographical location of the North, we see the epicenter of label category of Linguistic Features (Figure 3.32). Although the categories are distributed in the South and West as well, the most indicated area is in the Yankee territory. Since the two areas that are most salient in the perceptions of the respondents were the South and the North, in Figure 3.33 we created a composite map, based on the regions subsumed in the Southern and Yankee categories, to visualize the North/South divide.

The distribution of North versus South reflects the historical, cultural, and linguistic reality of the US. Recall that respondents were asked to describe the dialect landscape on the map that was given, and the major cultural divide of North versus South appears, revealing that the respondents see the speech of

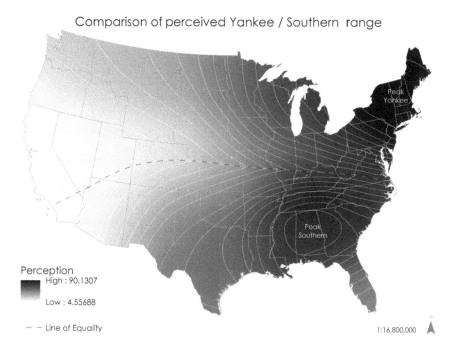

FIGURE 3.33 Comparison of perceived Yankee/Southern range.

these two regions as being in opposition as well. We often point to the Mason-Dixon Line as the divider, but in this map, the divide is actually much farther south than that. When respondents draw on stereotypes to make these distinctions, as some do, these stereotypes are anchored in approximate geographical locations. Because they are perceptions that we create out of the limited and variable amount of experiences we have with what we categorize as Southern or Northern (Yankee), their exact boundaries on the maps will vary. Hence, at the lowest level of agreement we see most of the country indicated. However, we do share a common cultural schema, based on, for example, the Civil War division between North and South, which allows us to pinpoint to an approximate, common location for both categories. In this way, we see that the structure of our planets of belief can hold very strong ideas about the South and North when confronted by the national-scale map. Some might even argue that the North can simply be defined as being NOT the South (and vice versa). These geographical anchors are clearly pretty strong for speakers to be able to pinpoint them consistently, sample after sample. Of course, the variation that we see in the maps is a realization of the various experiences we have in life, and lack of geographical knowledge, but the commonalities are nevertheless strong.

Returning now to the Northern categories Yankee (Figure 3.34) and Linguistic Features (Figure 3.35), we can see that the labels included in these categories reinforce individual ideas about speakers in the North.

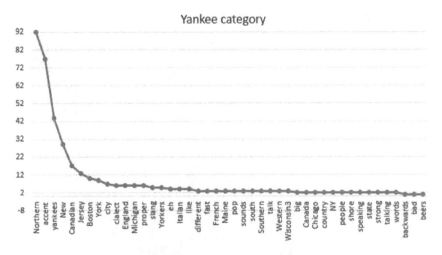

FIGURE 3.34 A-curve distribution of labels within the Yankee category.

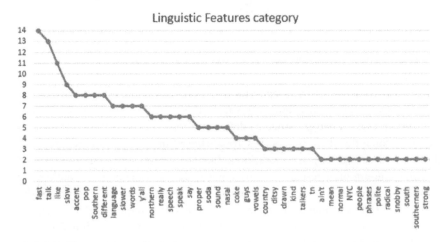

FIGURE 3.35 A-curve distribution of labels within the Linguistic Features category.

In the lemmatized list provided in Table 3.10 depicting the Yankee category, we find a view in which Yankees have a Northern accent; live in New York, New England, or Boston; and are sometimes Canadian. Such descriptions are not only superficial, but also show us that we really do not have to know much at all about a region or its people to point to it and label it.

This observation is also reinforced by the content of the Linguistic Features category in which respondents provided descriptions of how people speak. In Table 3.11, which consists of a lemmatized list of the labels from the Linguistic Features category, it becomes apparent that the speed at which people speak is

TABLE 3.10 Lemmas for the Yankee category

Northern	92	Maine	3
accent	77	pop	3
Yankees	44	sounds	3
New	29	South	3
Canadian	17	Southern	3
Jersey	13	talk	3
Boston	10	Western	3
York	9	Wisconsin	3
city	7	big	2
dialect	6	Canada	2
England	6	Chicago	2
Michigan	6	country	2
proper	6	NY	2
slang	5	people	2
Yorkers	5	shore	2
eh?	4	speaking	2
Italian	4	state	2
like	4	strong	2
different	3	talking	2
fast	3	words	2
French	3	backwards	1
beers	1	bad	1

TABLE 3.11 Lemmas for Linguistic Features category

fast	14	Coke	4
talk	13	Guys	4
like	11	Vowels	4
slow	9	Country	3
accent	8	Ditsy	3
pop	8	Drawn	3
Southern	8	Kind	3
different	8	Talkers	3
language	7	TN	3
slower	7	ain't	2
words	7	mean	2
y'all	7	normal	2
Northern	6	NYC	2
really	6	people	2
speech	6	phrases	2
speak	6	polite	2
say	6	radical	2
proper	5	snobby	2
soda	5	South	2
sound	5	Southerners	2
nasal	5	strong	2

an issue, as the words 'fast' and 'slow' were frequently used. There were also comparisons used, indicated by the word 'like'. Yet again, the content of the labels doesn't give us a detailed and complex idea about how people speak in the US.

What the content of the labels in the categories presented shows us is that, although people have something to say about the speech of others when they label perceptual maps at the national level, they do not provide much detail. What is interesting is that the level of detail doesn't seem to be connected to possible familiarity with particular speech. Regardless of whether speakers are native to the region in question or not, when asked for perceptions at a native level, they provide more stereotypes than they do any detailed description. Therefore, we may get a glimpse into one version of our planets of belief that does not seem to be very intrinsic. What it also implies is that this level of our perceptions does not reach very deep into the network of our beliefs. It seems that we are only scratching the surface when we are not zoomed in to what we believe about others, and therefore only bring out surface-level ideas.

Conclusion

The image of Planet USA that emerges from the labels and distributions of the perceptions is not a very detailed one. As shown in Figure 3.36, the respondents are relatively clear on the North/South division, but not so much with respect to the rest of the country.

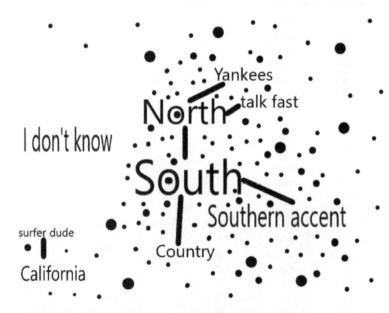

FIGURE 3.36 Hypothetical planet of beliefs for USA.

Figure 3.36 proposes a possible visualization of Planet USA. The dots represent ideas and beliefs that the respondents have about various parts of the country and their speakers. The words that are presented show the most frequent labels that emerged from the data. The empty space represents the gaps that the cognitive maps revealed in the creation of the result maps. This depiction confirms a relationship between the arrangement of the physical world and the cognitive construction we create, as described by Downs and Stea (2011:315) and discussed above.

If we consider the results in light of this view, we see that the cognitive maps are discontinuing surfaces, since there are vast areas that the respondents refer to as 'I don't know'. As proposed in Figure 3.36, these gaps can be represented as empty spaces to emphasize the difference between the various levels of engagement with beliefs respondents hold. As Preston (1989) explains, people are more willing to comment on areas that have stereotypes and caricatures attached to them, and that turns out to be true for Planet USA. We see this in the number of labels on the areas of the South and North and in the frequency of these labels. But what we see at the same time in the frequency is that there are a few common stereotypes brought in and used over and over again by the respondents. As was shown in multiple A-curves above, the way in which respondents label these two regions is very similar and frequent. So, we see that the Tennesseans have strong ideas about their region and the 'Yankee territory', but it is not very nuanced.

In describing how people perceive entities like the South, we might say that respondents who have dense and multiplex networks with other Southerners are more immersed in Southern culture and speech, which might impact how they describe and define it (Milroy 1987). Moreover, it seems that culturally and historically they have the most to say about the Northern region, but yet again in a frequent but unvaried way. Possibly, the reason for this is not the lack of ideas about these regions, but the scale at which they are being asked to showcase their attitudes. When the cartographic map given to respondents in a perceptual study displays the whole country, the level of detail might possibly be lost in the way the respondents present their ideas. So, yes there is a South and a North (and some other regions) in the country, but the lack of detail at this level of scale obscures the varied ways in which respondents differentiate between them. Therefore, it is only fitting to zoom into the maps and consider what the belief planet looks like if we get closer to the daily experience of our informants and ask about the regions they live in. Chapter 4 is an exploration of the Southern region as seen by Southerners.

References

Blaut, James M.; George F. McCleary; and America S. Blaut. 1970. Environmental mapping in young children. *Environment and Behavior* 2.335–49.

Bounds, Paulina, and Charles Sutherland. 2018. Perceptual basemaps reloaded: The role basemaps play in eliciting perceptions. *Journal of Linguistic Geography* 6.2.145–66.

Bradac, James J., and Randall Wisegarver. 1984. Ascribed status, lexical diversity, and accent: Determinants of perceived status, solidarity, and control of speech style. *Journal of Language and Social Psychology* 3.4.239–55.

Cramer, Jennifer. 2016. *Contested Southernness: The linguistic production and perception of identities in the borderlands.* Publication of the American Dialect Society 100. Durham, NC: Duke University Press.

Downs, Roger, and David Stea. 2011. Cognitive maps and spatial behavior: Process and products. *The map reader: Theories of mapping practice and cartographic representation*, 1st edition, ed. by Martin Dodge, Rob Kitchin and Kris Perkins, 312–17. Hoboken, NJ: John Wiley & Sons, Ltd.

Horvath, Barbara, and Ronald Horvath. 2003. A closer look at the constraint hierarchy: Order, contrast and geographical scale. *Language Variation and Change* 15.143–70.

Gould, Peter, and Rodney White. 1986. *Mental Maps*, 2nd edition. Boston, MA: Allen & Unwin.

Kretzschmar, William A., Jr. 2009. *The linguistics of speech.* Cambridge: Cambridge University Press.

Ladd, Florence. 1967. A note on 'The world across the street'. *Harvard Graduate School Regional Studies* 12.47–8.

Lambert, Wallace; R. Hodgson, R. Gardner; and S. Fillenbaum. I960. Evaluative reactions to spoken language. *Journal of Abnormal and Social Psychology* 60.44–51.

Milroy, Leslie. 1987. *Language and social networks.* New York: Blackwell.

Montgomery, Chris. 2012. The effect of proximity in perceptual dialectology. *Journal of Sociolinguistics* 16.5.638–68.

Niedzielski, Nancy, and Dennis R. Preston. 2000. *Folk linguistics.* Berlin: Mouton de Gruyter.

Preston, Dennis R. 1989. *Perceptual dialectology. Nonlinguists' views of areal linguistics.* Providence, RI: Fortis Publications.

Preston, Dennis R. 1996. Where the worst English is spoken. *Varieties of English around the world: Focus on the USA*, ed. by Edgar Schneider, 297–360. Amsterdam: John Benjamins.

Preston, Dennis R. 2015. The South: Still different. *New perspectives on language variety in the South: Historical and contemporary approaches*, ed. by Michael Picone and Catherine Davies, 311–27. Tuscaloosa, AL: University of Alabama Press.

Tamasi, Susan. 2003. Cognitive patterns of linguistic perceptions. University of Georgia, Diss.

4

SOUTHERN PLANETS

Hicks, hillbillies, and rednecks?

Introduction

As an entity, the Southern United States is completely enmeshed in half-truths and stereotypes. It is typecast as a backwards, racist, ignorant but pleasant purveyor of sweet tea and deep fried everything. For many Americans, the American South is a culture so embroiled in misinformation and mythologies that its true nature cannot be understood. This chapter zooms into specific beliefs about this linguistic corner of the world, and by applying the planets of belief metaphor, the language varieties spoken by inhabitants of the American South can be elucidated. What we find is that these varieties are variously categorized as 'dumb' but 'friendly', or 'slow, uneducated, and uncultured'. In this chapter, we thoroughly showcase the stereotypes held about Southerners (sometimes even held by Southerners), not only in terms of their language but more broadly as well.

To do so, we recall a specifically linguistic component of the planets of belief metaphor; in explaining that people are human beings *and* collections of atoms *but* not both at the same time (when thinking of how interactions take place), Carroll (2016) alludes to the notion that the language we use to describe our realities matters. He said, 'The most seductive mistake that we can be drawn into when dealing with multiple stories of reality is to mix up vocabularies appropriate to different ways of talking' (Carroll 2016:103). We have our own ways of describing the world around us, but these vocabularies are not unique to only one individual. Furthermore, these descriptions are more than descriptors; they also provide a glimpse into the ways in which we see the world. As such, the language that we use in our day-to-day lives has a tremendous power to shape our planets of beliefs. We want those planets to be comforting to us and to give us a feeling of being anchored to the world around us. We want to have a grasp on reality.

Here, we will discuss the reality of the Southern United States by using the planets of belief metaphor. What contributes to our assurance in our belief planets is the fact that other people share our beliefs. Those planets that are similar to other commonly possessed planets are called *habitable planets*, where one will find 'some shared convictions about evidence and rationality, as well as the actual information we have gathered about the world' (Carroll 2016:119). For example, if we perform a Google Image search of the word 'Southerner', the results showcased in Figure 4.1 reveal those commonalities that reflect shared perceptions. These perceptions are varied, but there is some consistency across the images, even if the picture is dichotomous:

> the picture of Southernness boils down to either distressed, cultured, and well-kept white women in need of rescuing, along with some gallant and handsome young men there to do so, or gun-toting, camouflage- or overall-wearing, rebel-flag-flying, toothless, mustachioed white men with vacant expressions.
>
> (Cramer, Tamasi, & Bounds 2018: 445)

This chapter is an examination of such habitable planets.

Where is the South?

Reed (1993:5) claimed,

> People more or less agree about which parts of the United States are in the South and which aren't … [this] tells us that the South is, to begin with, a

FIGURE 4.1 Google image search for 'Southerner'.

concept – and a shared one. It's an idea that people can talk about, use to orient themselves and each other.

If we were to examine the South from perspectives such as US Census definitions, participation in the Confederacy during the Civil War, or the proportion of Baptists in a given location (see Cramer & Preston 2018), we would see very similar pictures of the geographic location of the South.

Despite these similarities and the notion that the American South is a broadly shared construct, the question of where the South begins is one that has been the topic of much controversy and debate among Americans. How far West can you go and still be in the South? What about Missouri? Can we really count Washington, D.C.? As Kentuckians know, perhaps more than most, historical dividing lines like the Mason-Dixon Line or even the Ohio River, which Louisvillians once claimed made their city the 'gateway to the South', provide little definition to the modern-day South. In linguistics, we call such borderlands 'transition zones', and as will become clear, certain parts of the South are transitional, both in terms of linguistic production and perception.

If it is useful to have some kind of enumeration of the states that 'belong' in the region, it might be best to simply include those states found in Fridland and Bartlett's (2006) perceptual study as comprising the South, illustrated by the lighter shaded states in Figure 4.2. This definition essentially coincides with other definitions and is largely inclusive, even of border states like Kentucky and Oklahoma (though Maryland is excluded) that are often seen as contested members of the South. The map is comparable to those presented in Cramer and Preston (2018), and for our purposes, has the benefit of having been used in a previous perceptual study.

Interestingly, this general definition of the South aligns fairly well with linguistic production maps that seek to define the Southern dialect region. The

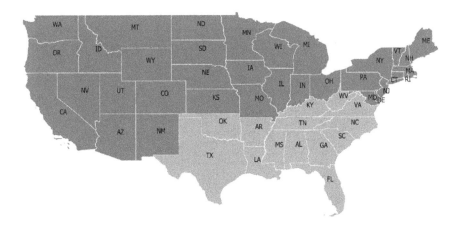

FIGURE 4.2 A general definition of the South, based on Fridland and Bartlett (2006).

map in Figure 4.3 was taken from Labov, Ash, and Boberg's (2006) *Atlas of North American English* (ANAE), in which the authors overlaid dialect regions from Carver (1987), based on lexical data collected for the *Dictionary of American Regional English* (DARE 2019), with their own findings based on sound systems at work in American dialects. As indicated in the text, 'There is a great deal of agreement in these two sets of isoglosses, particularly in the major divisions between Inland North, Midland, and South' (Labov et al. 2006:149). Focusing on the South in particular, the authors reported:

> The Midland/South boundary along the Ohio River also coincides for a good part of its length with the Lower North/Upper South boundary for Carver. In the eastward portion of this boundary, Carver follows the Mason-Dixon line, while the ANAE's northern limit of the South is far below that line. Florida is included in the South by Carver, but not by ANAE. The South proper for Carver does not include Texas, though another Carver isogloss, running north to south through New Mexico, comes close to the westward extension of the South in ANAE terms. Within the South, there is little agreement on the identification of sub-areas. The Inland South of ANAE does not appear on the Carver map as a distinct region and the Carver division between Upper and Lower South is not recognized in the ANAE data.
>
> (Labov et al. 2006:149)

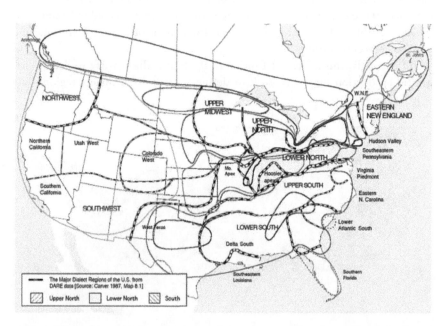

FIGURE 4.3   Map combining features from Carver (1987) and Labov et al. (2006). Source: Courtesy of Labov et al. (2006).

For the purposes of this book, however, it doesn't matter how linguists, census-makers, historians, preachers, or any other group define the South. The focus here is on language perceptions of everyday folks in their everyday lives, and our question must be centered on where people perceive the linguistic South. Perceptual dialectology (see Chapters 2 and 3) has a long history of showcasing perceptions of this entity; indeed, study after study (e.g. Preston 1989, 1993, 1996, 1999) has shown that nearly every American will draw a Southern dialect region in the draw-a-map task. The map in Figure 4.4 is an example from Cramer (2016a) that shows, for this participant, that the only region worth noting is a Southern one, and it extends much further than many similar perceptions of a Southern region (though perhaps it indicates a connection between Southernness and rurality in its inclusion of the southern parts of Illinois, Indiana, and Ohio). The informant includes the entirety of Kentucky in the region in full ownership of his own Southernness, saying (on a language attitudes survey about the region he drew) that he chose the name '[b]ecause when I talk to people up North [they] say I have some twang to my voice'.

Respondents in early work in perceptual dialectology drew similar regions. For example, the maps in Figures 4.5 and 4.6 are from Michigan and South Carolina (Preston 1996), respectively. Each contains a region called 'Southern(ers)', though the Michigan respondent has added the qualifier 'Hillbilly'. Unlike the map in Figure 4.4, these respondents include both coastal regions (Atlantic and Gulf) in their delimitations of the South. For the Michigan respondent, the South is one of several regions, but the addition of 'Hillbilly' plus the use of the word 'normal' in describing their own speech sets up a 'good vs. bad' English dichotomy. For the South Carolina respondent, the Southern region is much smaller, and the definition of the South as compared to 'Damn Yankees' is the only relevant distinction for the drawer of this map. This is not surprising: 'Southerners' maps much more often than Northerners' dichotomize North and South on a valued dimension' (Preston 1996:308).

FIGURE 4.4   Map showcasing a Southern dialect region. Source: Courtesy of Cramer (2016a).

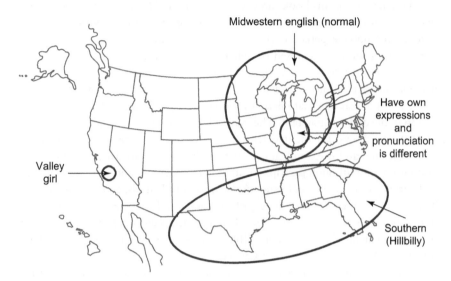

FIGURE 4.5 Map drawn by a Michigan respondent. Source: Courtesy of Preston (1996:307).

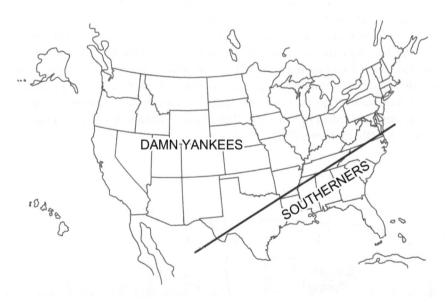

FIGURE 4.6 Map drawn by a South Carolina respondent. Source: Courtesy of Preston (1996:309).

The tradition of revealing a perceived Southern region continues in perceptual dialectology work carried out today and with Americans from various regions and backgrounds. The maps in Figures 4.7–4.9 are from, respectively, an Ohio respondent (Carmichael 2016), a Bostonian (Hartley 2005), and a woman from Michigan of Mexican heritage (Alfarez & Mason 2019). Together, they paint the picture of a very complex region. The region is built of several smaller regions, as in the 'Southern Drawl' and 'Country Southern' (in addition to numerous state-named dialect areas that *might* be considered Southern) of Figure 4.7. Or it is not, as in Figure 4.9, where only one dialect area is referred to as 'Southern'. The South excludes Texas, as in Figure 4.9. Or it does not, as in Figure 4.8, where two separate regions, one including Texas, are subsumed under two regions joined by the same label. It is connected to specific linguistic features like 'y'all', as in Figure 4.8. Or it is not, as in Figure 4.9, where every region except 'Southern' also includes the word 'accent' in the label. The inclusion of Figure 4.9 is particularly interesting, as many perceptual studies involve predominantly white respondent groups; the focus in Alfarez and Mason's (2019) work is on how people of other ethnicities view American regional dialects, and the study shows that while the South does not show up on every map for Latinx respondents, when it does appear, it resembles those drawn by white participants.

What has been shown in numerous perceptual studies is that maps of where the folk think Southern speech can be found do not neatly align with production maps of the American dialect landscape such as the one presented as Figure 4.3. The goal of these studies has been to better understand how individual

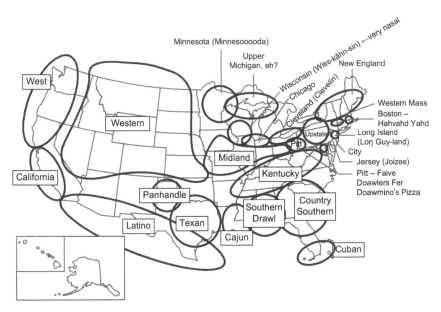

FIGURE 4.7 Map drawn by an Ohio respondent. Source: Courtesy of Carmichael (2016:307).

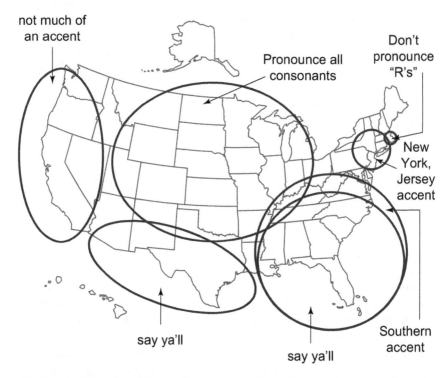

FIGURE 4.8 Map drawn by a Boston respondent. Source: Courtesy of Hartley (2005:393).

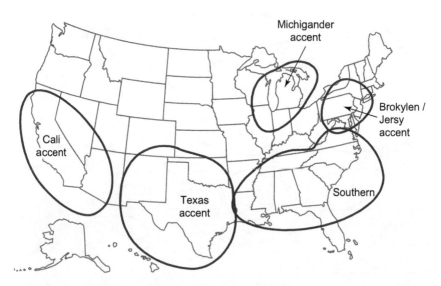

FIGURE 4.9 Map drawn by a Latina Michigan respondent. Source: Courtesy of Alfarez & Mason (2019:365).

respondents living in a particular dialect landscape view the changing nature of speech around them, and as such, their results can provide clues to linguists interested in changing patterns of production. It is unlikely that non-linguists experience their dialect landscapes in ways that are completely unrelated to the ways that linguists have described them (e.g. Niedzielski & Preston 2000), but this does not mean that perception- and production-based maps will be identical (e.g. Benson 2003). While early work in perceptual dialectology (e.g. Grootaers 1959; Sibata 1959, reprinted in Preston 1999) saw this kind of mismatch in perception and production as proof of the failure of the perceptual dialectology methodology, work carried out by Preston and others in the modern tradition of perceptual dialectology has viewed it as an opportunity to better account for language variation and change in progress.

And while the geographic delineations of the South might be fairly neutral, how it is described is not. Just as there can be agreement on the geographic expanse of the region, there can also be agreement on the labels used and the stereotypically negative ways of discussing its existence. If we recall the metaphor, we'll remember that our belief planets are not built on solid foundations and are instead held together in a self-fulfilling pattern. Because perceptions of Southernness often appear as unchanging and unquestionable, this metaphor provides an appropriate framework for understanding how Southern dialects have often been described as some of the worst American dialects (e.g. Preston 1996).

What's in a name?

Anyone who has named a child, a pet, or a plant knows how much thought and effort goes into selecting just the right moniker. And even those who have never named someone or something understand the importance of the process of naming, because they themselves have been named and either reap the benefits or suffer the consequences of the name chosen for them. Some people even choose names for themselves, either in the form of preferred nicknames and shortenings or by legally changing all or some portion of their name. Names and labels provide ways for people to categorize and identify (e.g. Hayakawa 1978). They influence how we react to people (e.g. Smith 1998) and how we see the world (e.g. Atkins-Sayre 2005).

Every new invention needs a name. Every newly discovered biological species needs a name. And, in language, whether new or not, every way of speaking needs a name. Just as we saw with linguistic mental maps, which do not always align with production maps, the names used to refer to linguistic entities can vary in similar ways. The names nonlinguists use to delineate varieties of American English, especially those associated with the American South, show considerable variation. Indeed, nonlinguists, even Southerners themselves, tend to use more derogatory labels for Southern varieties.

Overall, in examining how the South is labeled in various perceptual dialectology studies, we see unsurprising similarities across respondent groups. In
the 'Five Visions of America' study undertaken by Preston, in which all five
geographic groupings indicated a Southern dialect area, the typical (negative)
labels often used to delimit the South (labels like 'hillbilly' and 'hick') were 'used
with considerable frequency to indicate the entire area outlined as Southern'
(Preston 1989: 119; for more detail, see Chapter 3). Hartley and Preston (1999)
showed that these same labels were commonly used by their participants specifically when referring to the South Midland dialect area – a particularly interesting result given that some respondents in that study came from southern Indiana,
a part of the country that is either within or on the border of the South Midland
region that was being described. Our own work with these labels (plus 'redneck') in Kentucky (Cramer, Tamasi, & Bounds 2018) revealed that, when given
only a small portion of the country (in this case, just the Kentucky state outline),
the same kinds of distinctions made at more general levels ('hillbillies' vs. 'yankees', in a south–north US dichotomy) were reenacted at more specific levels to
indicate the same us vs. them mentality (non-Appalachians vs. Appalachians) in
the form of fractal recursivity (Irvine & Gal 2000). The choice of these labels
further serves to OTHER Appalachia, just as those same labels OTHER the Southern
dialect region as a whole in the dialect landscape of the United States.

Earlier work by Preston (1982) sought to categorize these kinds of labels in a
topical fashion, enumerating 11 different types of labels given to regional varieties, with the following topics serving as the main categories by which labels can
be classified: area (geographic, topographic, political), sound, identity, ethnicity,
media (pop culture references), attributes, standardness, distribution, intelligibility,
variety, and extended commentary. Using these categories, Hartley and Preston
(1999) found that area was the most commonly utilized category for labels, though
sound, identity, and variety were frequently used as well. With regard to the South,
they showed that not only was it the most commonly labeled region, but it was also
more likely than not to be given a negative or neutral label and was rarely given a
positive label, even by Southerners. In what follows, we present our own findings
with respect to the kinds of labels used by Southerners in labeling the dialect region
that coincides with the geographic expanse known as the Southern United States.

Beyond 'hick', 'hillbilly', and 'redneck', Kentuckians use numerous labels to
describe the Southern dialect region. The original project for which the data
was collected (Cramer 2010) sought to understand how Louisvillians represent
their own dialect in terms of regionality in a map that included the larger region
around Kentucky (see Figure 4.10). The dataset for this study consisted of 23
maps and a total of 94 individual labels for regions that were eventually subsumed under 11 overarching categories. An analysis of all labels produced in that
study, wherein each label could be given two major label categories, based on a
smaller set of categories than Preston (1982), is presented in Table 4.1. Dividing
this among the 11 overarching categories for the regions delineated in Cramer
(2010), we find the labels to be divided as in Table 4.2. While Geography and

FIGURE 4.10 Basemap for regional perceptions in Kentucky. Source: Courtesy of Cramer (2010).

TABLE 4.1 Overall frequency of labels (Cramer 2010)

Type	Frequency	Percentage
Culture (e.g. 'Country', 'Rural')	13	10%
Economics (e.g. 'Poor Southern Hick')	1	1%
Ethnicity (e.g. 'Mixed-up')	4	3%
Geography (e.g. 'Southern', 'Kentucky')	71	53%
Language (e.g. 'Southern twang', 'Hillbilly twang')	35	26%
Personality (e.g. 'Redneck', 'Hillbilly')	10	7%
TOTAL	134	100%

TABLE 4.2 Types of labels by region (Cramer 2010)

	Culture	Economics	Ethnicity	Geography	Language	Personality
Appalachia	9.5%	–	–	42.9%	23.8%	23.8%
Cajun/ Creole	–	–	60.0%	–	40.0%	–
Chicago	–	–	–	88.9%	11.1%	–
Georgia	40.0%	–	–	60.0%	–	–
Kentucky	33.3%	–	–	33.3%	11.1%	22.2%
Louisville/ Lexington	16.7%	–	8.3%	58.3%	16.7%	–
Mid-Atlantic	–	–	–	36.4%	45.5%	18.2%
Midwest	20.0%	–	–	70.0%	10.0%	–
Northern	0.0%	0.0%	0.0%	61.5%	38.5%	0.0%
Southern	6.1%	3.0%	0.0%	60.6%	30.3%	0.0%
Tennessee	0.0%	0.0%	0.0%	33.3%	50.0%	16.7%

Language predominate overall, labels for the South are more divided across label types. References to any geographic locations (e.g. state/city names, regional references like 'Southern') or geographic features (e.g. mountains) were included in the Geography category. For the South, this obviously included labels like 'Southern', as well as references to specific states and cities, but it also included references to the notion of a 'deep' South, something distinct from other Southern places but also as an entity that likely shares features with other regions called 'South'. In terms of the Economics category, there was only one label – 'Poor South Hick' – indicating that, despite a general sense that some people connect ways of talking to class and wealth, the category seems to be less productive for these map labelers. The Ethnicity category was primarily reserved for discussions of the Cajun or Creole language variety that participants connected to Louisiana (interestingly, this state was not included in the map, but participants circled parts of Mississippi and Alabama to indicate where this language can be found). The Culture, Personality, and Language categories, however, were more intriguing for the Southern dialect area.

Within the category of Culture, we included references to 'urban', 'rural', and 'country' varieties. These words (and the descriptions of their use on the language attitudes survey) seemed to indicate something about how the people live in a given area. In the open-ended responses, for example, we found several references to things like 'Coal influenced culture' and 'Heritage rooted in a particular culture', indicating that the participants who offered these observations might see culture as a determiner of language or language variety. Relatedly, the Personality category mainly included labels that seemed to indicate the types of people who speak the variety, including words like 'hillbilly', 'hick', and 'redneck', as well as explicit references to people, like 'Mountain people'. Interestingly, the majority of these references to personality traits were used as labels for the Appalachia region. This suggests that these personality traits loom large in the belief planets of these Louisvillians in describing their eastern neighbors. It serves as a way to differentiate themselves, as if to say, 'Yes, Louisville is in Kentucky, but it's not like THAT kind of Kentucky'.

References to types of language varieties (e.g. dialect, accent, slang, etc.) or to how the language in the given area is produced (e.g. discussions of pronunciation, word choice, prosody, etc.) were included in the Language category. For the South, this included references to accents, drawls, and twangs, as well as indications that the language variety is 'slow'. Indeed, these mentions of language types were so pervasive across the entire dataset (which might be expected because of the task), we also counted the words that appeared most often in the labels used, including words like 'accent' and 'drawl', as in Table 4.3. If we again distribute these by overarching category, as in Table 4.4, we see these terms being used heavily for both the Southern and the Appalachian region, as well as for other places that fall within the geographical scope of the South, such as Tennessee, Georgia, and Kentucky.

TABLE 4.3 Overall common word frequency in labels (Cramer 2010)

Word	Frequency
Accent	15
Country	7
Drawl	5
Hick	4
Hillbilly	7
Mountain	5
Twang	5

TABLE 4.4 Overall common word frequencies by region (Cramer 2010)

	Accent	Country	Drawl	Hick	Hillbilly	Mountain	Twang
Appalachia	2	2	1	1	4	4	1
Cajun/ Creole	–	–	–	–	–	–	–
Chicago	1	–	–	–	–	–	–
Georgia	–	2	–	–	–		
Kentucky	–	1	–	2	–	–	1
Louisville/Lexington	–	–	1	–	–	–	–
Mid-Atlantic	3	–	–	–	2	–	–
Midwest	1	1	–	–	–	–	–
Northern	3	–	–	–	–	–	–
Southern	4	1	3	1	–	–	1
Tennessee	1	–	–	–	1	–	2

We find the distribution of the words 'drawl' and 'twang' to be of interest; despite the fact that many people use these words as synonyms, the range of use is wide. Some users attach 'drawl' to the language of the Appalachia, Louisville/ Lexington, and the South as a whole, while 'twang' can reference Appalachia and the South, as well as Kentucky and Tennessee. Similarly, words like 'hick' and 'hillbilly' seem to be related, as they are both applied to Appalachia in these data. We find 'hick' used to describe the Kentucky and Southern regions, and the label 'hillbilly' is used to identify the Mid-Atlantic and Tennessee regions. The general connection between 'hillbilly' and mountains is seen in these choices, but if this is the case, why are there no hillbillies in Kentucky? And if the mountains themselves are part of the defining characteristics of these other regions, why does the word 'mountain' only appear in descriptions of Appalachia?

When it comes to the sentiment attached to the labels chosen, we find that the vast majority of labels used for any region were fairly neutral, especially when considering the explanations people provided for why they selected a specific label for a certain region. Table 4.5 reveals the overall frequency of positive, negative, and neutral labels from our analysis, and Table 4.6 shows how their use can be compared across the overarching categories. Only the Mid-Atlantic and Southern regions garnered labels that can be outwardly described as positive. These include 'Proper' for the Mid-Atlantic region and 'Southern Belle' for the South. While these data feature no outwardly hostile labels, words like 'hick', 'drawl', and even 'country' are described in ways that reveal they were selected because they potentially carry the negative connotations associated with the region and its language variety.

If we zoom into the state-only map, as we did in Cramer, Tamasi, and Bounds (2018), in addition to the finding that Appalachia is seen as being the most representative of Southernness (negatively defined) within the state of Kentucky, we also see interesting patterns in the labels used. Table 4.7 shows the 20 most common words that were found in the labels used to describe the state in terms of linguistic variation. If we only compare how the words 'accent' and 'drawl' are used for these groups, Table 4.8 shows how these are distributed among the five overarching categories determined in that study. As found in previous work (e.g. Cramer 2016b), Northern and Central Kentucky are exempted from the more derogatory label 'drawl', fermenting their place as the economic and linguistic

TABLE 4.5 Labels as negative, neutral, or positive

Category	Frequency
Negative	32
Neutral	58
Positive	4
TOTAL	94

TABLE 4.6 Labels as negative, neutral, or positive by region

	Negative	Neutral	Positive
Appalachia	53.3%	46.7%	–
Cajun/Creole	–	100.0%	–
Chicago	12.5%	87.5%	–
Georgia	40.0%	60.0%	–
Kentucky	66.7%	33.3%	–
Louisville/Lexington	12.5%	87.5%	–
Mid–Atlantic	28.6%	42.9%	28.6%
Midwest	28.6%	71.4%	–
Northern	37.5%	62.5%	–
Southern	28.6%	61.9%	9.5%
Tennessee	60.0%	40.0%	–

TABLE 4.7 Overall common word frequency in labels for state-only maps

Word	Frequency	Word	Frequency
Northern	105	Redneck	30
Southern	101	Appalachian	29
Country	78	Central	28
Accent	55	Mountain	24
Western	50	Proper	21
City	46	Louisville	20
Eastern	45	Midwestern	18
Hillbilly	44	Normal	18
Number	37	Mix	16
Hick	34	Drawl	14

TABLE 4.8 Distribution of 'accent' and 'drawl' for state-only maps by region

	Accent	Drawl
Central Kentucky/Bluegrass	3.9%	0%
Eastern Kentucky	3.9%	1.6%
Northern Kentucky	6.6%	0%
Southern Kentucky	4.8%	2.4%
Western Kentucky	3.8%	3.8%

golden triangle within the state. Taken together with the results concerning the labels 'hicks', 'hillbillies', and 'rednecks' in our previous work, the picture of the dialect landscape within Kentucky is clearly divided in a way that suggests certain segments of the state COUNT as Southern, whereas others are more peripherally Southern. We believe this is further recognition of the border status of the state. Situated as it is in the crossroads of America, and as the 'front porch' of the South, Kentucky suffers from a great deal of linguistic insecurity that gets played out at both the regional and statewide levels in these tasks.

Turning to the view from Tennessee, we find some other interesting patterns. Table 4.9 contains a list of the most common label types used. When all labels were collected from the 180 maps depicting only Tennessee, a total of 601 labels were given; in all, only 51 (or 8%) areas indicated on the maps were not given any label. The average map contained three labels. There were ten major categories of labels, and Table 4.9 also includes the frequencies for each category. As with the Kentucky maps, Southern is a popular though unsurprising category of labels for Tennesseeans. While references to speed and urbanity appeared in some Kentucky maps, these categories are more productive for Tennessee respondents.

The most common label category, Southern, can be further broken down, as in Table 4.10. For Tennesseeans, their home state is 'Southern' first, with 104

TABLE 4.9 All Tennessee labels

Name of the label category	Number of labels in the category
Southern	174
Geographical Names	106
Miscellaneous	94
Urban	61
No Label	51
Gangster	36
Regional	35
Redneck	18
Speed	15
Proper	10

TABLE 4.10 Types of Southern labels

Category: Southern	Frequency
Southern	104
Country	70
Accent	48
People	11
Heavy	11

instances of that specific label used for the state, with 'Country' coming in second at 70. We believe this reveals a fractal recursivity similar to that of 'hick', 'hillbilly', and 'redneck'; it appears that Tennesseeans see their state as 'Southern' in the larger national perceptions (see Chapter 3), but when a map is zoomed into the state alone, some portions of the state are 'Southern' while others are only 'Country', a label often used in such exercises as a derogatory moniker. It is as if Tennessee has various degrees of Southernness, just as the Kentucky maps reveal. We believe this indicates that respondents have schemas of Southernness, with different ideas about its constitution depending on the different scales of regional observational artifacts. These different scales can perhaps be seen as different particles of the perceptual planet.

The idea of Southernness is also present in the second most frequent category: Geographical Names. All labels that had a geographical location as a referent are included in this category, with Memphis, Nashville, Knoxville, and Cookeville emerging as the top locations pointed out by the informants, as seen in Table 4.11. This trend indicates that observational artifacts can be attached not only to regions but also to specific cities. Not all cities in Tennessee showed up frequently, as the only other three cities that appeared were Chattanooga (5 times), Murfreesboro (4 times), and Crossville (3 times). Thus, it seems that there are localities that receive more recognition than others for having some

TABLE 4.11 Types of Geographical Names labels

Category: Geographical Names	Frequency
Memphis	24
Nashville	23
Country	19
Southern	15
Accent	14
Knoxville	12
Cookeville	11

sort of characteristic speech. This fact is intrinsically linked to the notion that the most commonly used labels overall are Southern or Country, as the collocation analysis above revealed. The schema of Tennessee gets more complex here. At the state level, Tennessee is Southern, but when those labels are used on the state-only map, respondents point to specific localities in the state that are actually 'Southern' and others that are 'Country'.

However, what makes this Tennessee picture even more complex is the second most frequent category of labels: Urban. The manner in which these labels are divided and their frequencies are shown in Table 4.12. Here we find that the respondents distinguish the cities and urban areas as places where one might find a specific way of talking. The Geographical Names category gives the impression that these urban areas are still country and Southern, which is not a typical combination in these kinds of research tasks. However, in the Urban category, the words 'accent', 'talk', and 'like' are used to point out that these urban areas are less country than the rest. So, which is it? Are these cities Southern and country, or are they less Southern and country than the rest of the state?

Such a contrasting distribution may point to several factors. For one, it shows us that the variation in the perceptual planets is great, and not only between people, but even within their own planets. It may indicate that our various experiences and beliefs about a place might not always neatly fit with other competing beliefs. Indeed, it is possible to have contrasting and contradicting ideas about a place – you can believe that people in cities are 'better' (by some metric), while still saying people in SOME cities (like those in the South) are not so much better

TABLE 4.12 Types of Urban labels

Category: Urban	Frequency
City	47
Urban	15
Accent	11
Talk	10
Like	9

by the same metric. Labels and their distributions are a way of getting a glimpse into what beliefs we may hold about the world around us, allowing us a way to peer into the perceptual planets we create. Their distribution on perceptual maps provides us a way to describe the mental space in which we enact these beliefs.

This already messy picture is further confounded by our Tennessee respondents apparently having a problem agreeing on which parts of the state are Southern and which are not. Part of the design of this experiment was to test the impact of the type of map given (that is, what information was included on each map varied, such that some maps included more or less geographic, political, and other information; see Bounds and Sutherland 2018 for a broader analysis). When we look at the six different maps, as in Figure 4.11, the areas indicated do not really look all that similar. On a map featuring county lines, East Tennessee and part of Middle Tennessee count as Southern. On the map featuring only the capital city and the empty map, the highest level of 'Southern' agreement is located in the northern part of Tennessee. On the maps featuring interstates and topography, the southern part of Tennessee is indicated as being the most Southern. Finally, in the map featuring several major towns in Tennessee, there are pockets of high-level agreement anchored in some of the bigger towns indicated on the map, like Nashville, Knoxville, and Chattanooga. As we can see on the composite maps for the different map types, the variability of the distribution of the Southern areas may indicate that the kind of information on the maps doesn't really matter. The respondents seem to designate a Southern region based on the shape of their own perceptual planets. Moreover, we can assume that the respondents have more variable and personal experiences with the state than with the whole country (as seen in Chapter 3). Hence, the higher level of variability in their responses is visible in these maps. In all, it is possible that the border phenomenon experienced

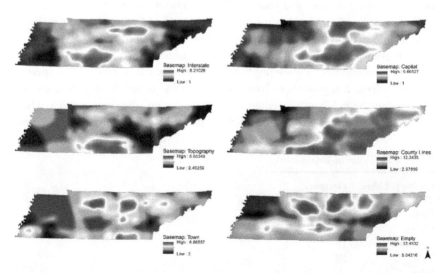

FIGURE 4.11   Six different impressions of Southern.

by Kentucky residents is actually just the same variation in schema found in the Tennessee case. It's not likely that Tennesseans feel that their overall Southern status is in jeopardy. Rather, just as Kentuckians relegated the negative notions of Southernness to the eastern portion of the state, Tennessee respondents simply see the world a little differently when the map is a bit smaller.

Finally, we can also examine the view of the South from Georgia. In a novel exploration of the question 'Is there a way in which we think about language in the South that makes it so common in folk linguistic perceptions?', Tamasi (2003) used a pile sort method (see Chapter 2) to discover the ways in which people separate individual states into various groupings. A cluster analysis showed that Georgia participants placed Kentucky, West Virginia, Virginia, North Carolina, South Carolina, Georgia, Alabama, Mississippi, Louisiana, Arkansas, and Tennessee together as the Southern region at a clustering level of .25, meaning that there is minimal similarity among these states, but enough to distinguish them separately from the rest of the US. Raise the level to .50, representing an increased perceived similarity between clustered states, and the Southern region loses Arkansas, Louisiana, West Virginia, and Virginia. However, one of the more interesting findings in this research is that using this specific method eliminated the need for spatial interference, and very few participants in that study sorted states with 100% maintenance of geospatial considerations, indicating that the importance of the geographic distribution of varieties may be diminished by changing the task.

While Tamasi (2003) did not feature labels like the Kentucky and Tennessee data presented here did, respondents were also asked to sort states in terms of social characteristics and provided descriptions of voices using regional and social information. Results indicated that people rely heavily on four very basic categories in sorting places and people by their ways of speaking: regional information, social information, personal experience, and linguistic input. Respondents preferred to describe states as being more or less standard, as more or less local, and as good or bad. The interactions of these categories, however, is less basic. As Tamasi (2003: 170) reported, '[A] perception of local speech may lead to an overlapping perception of good speech'. In other words, there is a complex, multi-layered network of knowledge that is accessed when people think about language.

As mentioned above, when states were sorted by regional dialect, we found that non-contiguous dialect regions were quite common. For example, in Figure 4.12, we see many such combinations, with this respondent, like others, placing states like New York and Florida in the same dialect groups. With regard to this particular grouping, respondents often reported an observation to the effect of everybody who retires in New York moves to Florida so that people in New York and Florida sound the same.

The inclusion of regional information in these kinds of categorizations is perhaps unsurprising. The United States is a big country, and we often use region to discuss different issues, for example, the weather, politics, etc. Through

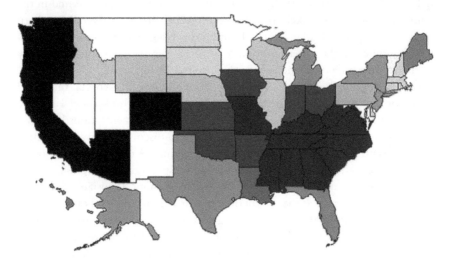

FIGURE 4.12 Georgia respondent grouping of states. Each shade represents a different dialect group.

categorization, we are able to discriminate between large amounts of information. Categories make knowledge manageable. For example, with telephone numbers, we don't memorize all ten numbers at once. We put them into chunks in order to more efficiently and accurately access the information. As Conforti (2001:1–2) explains:

> regions bring geographic and cultural order to the sprawling continental United States. Regions help make America geographically comprehensible. Regions are not only concrete geographic domains but also conceptual places. Humans define regions; they are not geographic entities that define themselves. Regional identity is not simply an organic outcome of human interaction with the physical environment – the geology and climate, for example – of a particular place. Regions are real places but also historical artifacts whose cultural boundaries shift over time.

Similarly, with dialect regions, we rely on regional categories to express our folk linguistic knowledge. If we look at region as it pertains to Southern speech, the South was the main region identified by Georgians in this task. After arriving at an understanding of what respondents perceived and what they thought about these perceptions, the next step was to ask if there is some underlying set of conditions that connect the two matters. The answer, which can also be seen in examining the Kentucky and Tennessee data above, is that the connection between what is perceived and how it is perceived is simply human nature. As Tamasi (2003:174) said, 'Because, as humans, we think about the world differently and process information through our own personal experiences, there are many interesting variations of these perceptions that stem from the same patterns of categorization'. In this book, we are representing these interesting variations in terms of linguistic planets of belief. In what follows, we will attempt to capture these varying planets while getting a specific sense of why the South plays such an important role in these depictions of language variation in the United States.

Why is the South so important?

In short, there is a common perception by both linguists and nonlinguists that the American South is, was, and forever will be a different linguistic situation. The broader role of the South within the larger context of the United States is multifaceted, but when it comes to language, it seems to serve one purpose: 'as a foil to [Standard American English]' (Preston 1997:311). There just seems to be something special about language in the South.

Perhaps this notion can be represented in a wide-view perceptual planet, like the one presented in Figure 4.13. Here, we focus on the language component of the standardness-localness scale, fully recognizing that the dots represented here may indicate items other than those that are language-related. The Georgia respondents were explicit in this, but both the Kentucky and Tennessee respondents also note standardness and localness as important components of their views on language. There is overlap, such that local things can be standard and vice versa, but there are also ways in which these items are held as separate. In much of the perceptual dialectology research, notions of correctness and degrees of difference have figured prominently, such that one's home area is usually the first area acknowledged, followed closely by those places that are disparaged. Yet, people do not possess one style, or one way of talking, and the movement between national standards, local standards, and more colloquial or vernacular ways of

FIGURE 4.13 Wide-view of the standard–local dimension.

speaking is fluid. With this notion of the mythical single style speaker in mind, we turn to Southern speech, which is conceived of by many outsiders as a slow and perhaps grammarless way of speaking. It seems impossible to imagine, given the idea that people can modulate their speech based on any number of characteristics (e.g. formality, location, addressee), that Southerners would be any different, yet the description of their speech is so consistent as to paint the picture of speakers incapable of variation. Do Southerners recognize and use a local standard? Do they position themselves as occasional speakers of some national standard? Do their own impressions of their language, their sense of belonging, and their belief planets align with those outside of the South? We will focus on the Southern belief planet, of Southerners themselves, revealing a replication of these same dimensions at a more regional and even local level.

Our work is meant to showcase that there are patterns to folk perceptions of language. We explore not only how folk knowledge of language is cognitively categorized but also how folk perceptions and knowledge of language structure and use are not always clearly connected. Indeed, the linguistic role of the South, even (or especially) among Southerners themselves, is quite complex. When it comes to regional identity, Southerners often find themselves in a love–hate relationship. Some of this is tied to external forces; as Cramer and Preston (2018:337) said,

> The southern United States is unique in that, as a subculture within the larger tapestry of Americanness, Southernness is something everyone knows something, everything, and nothing about. With or without real exposure to Southernness, a picture of the South has been constructed in the national imagination, and this image is at least bifurcated—it is Gone with the Wind, Southern belles, mint juleps, and front porch swings, and, simultaneously, it is Beverly Hillbillies.

Indeed, this same bifurcation can be said to exist in language perceptions as well. A great deal of work in sociolinguistics, linguistic anthropology, social psychology, and elsewhere has highlighted the 'friendly but stupid' stereotype of the Southern accent. In Figure 4.14, we have attempted a representation of a belief planet that takes this bifurcation into consideration. It also aligns with the standardness–localness dimension of Figure 4.13, in that we have zoomed into this dichotomy and mapped notions of correctness and pleasantness, two of the key social characteristics explored in perceptual dialectology research, onto these ideas of standardness and localness. This is a representation of the kinds of data we have discussed so far, and it acknowledges the struggle that many (though not all) Southerners experience with respect to balancing their various linguistic selves.

For example, if we look at the Kentucky data, the border nature of the state appears to play a role in linguistic perceptions (cf. Cramer 2016a). When thinking about the South as a whole and how Kentucky fits into the region, the active and agentive recognition of this border allows Kentuckians to portray themselves as being both this AND that, not wholly one or the other, but definitely NOT the

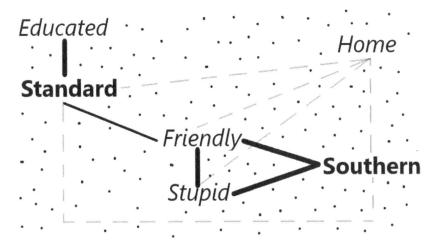

FIGURE 4.14 Theoretical zoomed–in Southern belief planet.

negative stereotypes of the South that are common in the media. If they have to acknowledge that those stereotypes are applied in the larger American conscious-ness to their state, Kentuckians (even ones in Eastern Kentucky) will pass them on to Appalachia. Through the presentation of their linguistic ideologies in this way, they have firmly held on to their belief planets. Casting Appalachia in a negative light provides a way for those who do not associate themselves with Southernness to express that they believe other components of their state may, in fact, be Southern. Kentuckians' OTHER is Appalachia, allowing them to claim Southernness without claiming the negative stereotypes associated with the OTHER.

As we have shown elsewhere (Cramer, Tamasi, & Bounds 2018), this appears to be an example of fractal recursivity (Irvine & Gal 2000), in which respondents are enacting the larger, national dichotomy of North vs. South at a state level. Specifically, the labels 'hick', 'hillbilly', and 'redneck', and all their negative con-notations, are being used mostly to describe the eastern portion of the state. These labels are seen broadly to refer to Southern identities, and their use almost exclusively in Appalachia serves to distance other Kentuckians from the nega-tive stereotypes, to put Eastern Kentucky in its place at the bottom of the state's linguistic hierarchy, and to place the blame of the nation's negative perception of the state squarely on Appalachians. A very specific example of a belief planet for these terms can be seen in Figure 4.15, which looks much like a Venn diagram, where each dot represents some sentiment that goes along with each label. For Kentuckians, the only group that fits all three categories of 'hick', 'hillbilly', and 'redneck' is Appalachian Eastern Kentucky. Its location at the confluence of these three ideas marks it as uniquely characterized by all the beliefs that are entailed by their inclusion with these labels. As we saw in the data, those beliefs are generally rather derogatory.

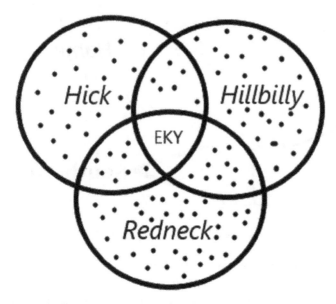

FIGURE 4.15   Hick, hillbilly, and redneck belief planet.

Who cares?

Despite our desire to be in a comfortable place, sometimes we encounter people, have experiences, or make observations that do not fit with our planets. For example, if our belief planet automatically links Southern speech features with a lack of standardized education, then what happens to our planet when we hear a college professor say 'y'all'? Such a discordant belief is potentially problematic because of the intrinsic notion of education associated with being a college professor. In such circumstances, we are met with two main options: we can pause, reconsider our beliefs, and adjust them to accommodate this new encounter, or we can react by defending our planets.

The first option here is difficult. Adjusting our belief planets is hard work that our efficient minds don't want to do. Instead, many choose to simply deny the reality, mark the not-quite-fitting speaker as just an anomaly, or, through cognitive dissonance, manipulate the particles of the planet so that the experience is forced to fit. Perhaps we even write the professor off as not as intelligent as they should be, given their status. We know this happens with commercial pilots; a 2018 study found that pilots who had Southern accents, particularly Texan ones, instilled less confidence among passengers with regard to their flying abilities (see Erskine 2018). Similarly, research on evaluations of teachers suggests that any 'non-standard' English accent, including a Southern one, results in a perceived lower level of credibility (e.g. Ballard & Winke 2017), revealing the fact that social and linguistic information are integrated in the perception of speech and identities of speakers (e.g. McGowan 2015). In the college classroom, then, students may adjust things like terms of address (some female professors in the South, and elsewhere, report getting called Ms. instead of Dr. by innocently ignorant and outwardly hostile students alike) or teacher evaluation scores (some Southern-sounding professors believe students have given them lower scores simply because of their speech) to reveal their belief planets about connections between education and dialect.

Changing our beliefs has been described in this way:

> The most violent revolutions in an individual's beliefs leave most of his old order standing. Time and space, cause and effect, nature and history, and one's own biography remain untouched. New truth is always a go-between, a smoother-over of transitions. It marries old opinion to new fact so as ever to show a minimum of jolt, a maximum of continuity.
>
> (James 1907:61)

This assertion suggests that our planets do not have it in their nature to change abruptly, and any change needs to be rejected or accepted only very gradually, otherwise such a deconstruction could be seen as catastrophic to our planets.

Indeed, it seems that we have developed fairly robust processes for safeguarding our belief planets. As Carroll says:

> We shouldn't overestimate people's rationality or willingness to look at new evidence as objectively as possible. For better or for worse, planets eventually develop highly sophisticated defense mechanisms. When you realize that you are holding two beliefs that are in conflict with each other, psychologists refer to the resulting discomfort as cognitive dissonance. It's a sign that there is something not completely structurally sound about your planet of belief. Unfortunately, human beings are extremely good at maintaining the basic makeup of their planets, even under very extreme circumstances … Human beings are not nearly as coolly rational as we like to think we are. Having set up comfortable planets of belief, we become resistant to altering them, and develop cognitive biases that prevent us from seeing the world with perfect clarity. We aspire to be perfect Bayesian abductors, impartially reasoning to the best explanation—but most often we take new data and squeeze it to fit with our preconceptions.
>
> (2016:111–12)

As it is, we tend to give higher priority to the notions, biases, and beliefs that benefit us in some way. These are the proposals that are in favor of the things that we *want* to be true. Maybe they make us look better or smarter. In general, they confirm the worldview we already hold. They can be used to reinforce what our beliefs already say about other speakers. Returning to the use of 'y'all' being linked to lack of education, when we encounter a speaker that uses 'y'all' AND no other signs indicating a high level of education (unlike the professor example), we believe our ideas about Southerners have been confirmed. We might even think we are really good at 'spotting the Southerner'. We probably also ignored that this person used other variants that don't necessarily point to their being a Southerner, but unless it benefits us to change this idea, we ignore these other signs. That may be what happens with the professor; even though we should expect high levels of education before ever hearing a professor speak a word, perhaps listeners are so struck by the disconnect between what they believe is supposed to be true (educated) and what they are hearing ('uneducated' language use) that they ignore the other information they have. These biases (specifically the confirmation bias, for example) work in a selective way so that our minds keep what fits our planets of belief and maintain the story that we continuously tell ourselves. The way our mind creates the narrative of self and of the world around us is crucial for our sanity and our ideas of what is 'real'.

So the most reasonable and obvious answer to the question of 'who cares?' is simply this: everyone. Since we all interact with speakers of various dialects and languages, it is important for everyone to be aware of the beliefs they hold with respect to various ways of speaking. The reason that we (the authors) study language attitudes is exactly because we recognize that humans are natural categorizers, and it is important that everyone recognizes when the way in which we categorize people is discriminatory. Being in the South, we have encountered countless stories of dialect discrimination (see Chapter 6). It is our hope that this research about linguistic perceptions of Southernness can bring to light some of the cognitive connections people make without even being aware of them.

References

Alfarez, Gabriela G., and Alexander Mason. 2019. Ethnicity and perceptual dialectology: Latino awareness of U.S. regional dialects. *American Speech* 94.352–79.

Atkins-Sayre, Wendy. 2005. Naming women: The emergence of "Ms." as a liberatory title. *Women and Language* 28.8–16.

Ballard, Laura, and Paula Winke. 2017. Students' attitudes towards English teachers' accents: The interplay of accent familiarity, comprehensibility, intelligibility, perceived native speaker status, and acceptability as a teacher. *Second language pronunciation assessment: Interdisciplinary perspectives*, ed. by Talia Isaacs and Pavel Trofimovich, 121–40. Bristol: Multilingual Matters.

Benson, Erica J. 2003. Folk linguistic perceptions and the mapping of dialect boundaries. *American Speech* 78.307–30.

Carmichael, Katie. 2016. Place-linked expectations and listener awareness of regional accents. *Awareness and control in sociolinguistic research*, ed. by A.M. Babel, 152–76. Cambridge: Cambridge University Press.

Carroll, Sean. 2016. *The big picture: On the origins of life, meaning, and the universe itself.* New York: Penguin.

Carver, Craig M. 1987. *American regional dialects: A word geography.* Ann Arbor, MI: University of Michigan Press.

Conforti, Joseph A. 2001. *Imagining New England: Explorations of regional identity from the Pilgrims to the mid-twentieth century.* Chapel Hill, NC: University of North Carolina Press.

Cramer, Jennifer. 2010. *The effect of borders on the linguistic production and perception of regional identity in Louisville, Kentucky.* Champaign, IL: University of Illinois, Ph.D. diss..

Cramer, Jennifer. 2016a. *Contested Southernness: The linguistic production and perception of identities in the borderlands.* Publication of the American Dialect Society 100. Durham, NC: Duke University Press.

Cramer, Jennifer. 2016b. Rural vs. urban: Perception and production of identity in a border city. *Cityscapes and perceptual dialectology: Global perspectives on non-linguists' knowledge of the dialect landscape,* ed. by J. Cramer and C. Montgomery, 27–54. Language and Social Life 5. Berlin: Mouton de Gruyter.

Cramer, Jennifer, and Dennis R. Preston. 2018. Introduction: Changing perceptions of Southernness. *American Speech* 93.337–43.

Cramer, Jennifer; Susan Tamasi; and Paulina Bounds. 2018. Southernness and our linguistic planets of belief: The view from Kentucky. *American Speech* 93.445–70.

Dictionary of American Regional English (DARE). 2019. *Digital DARE.* https://www.daredictionary.com/.

Erskine, Chris. 2018. 'Hey y'all' — passengers don't trust pilots with Southern accents nearly as much as Midwestern pilots. *Los Angeles Times.* https://www.latimes.com/travel/la-tr-airline-pilots-accents-20180921-story.html.

Fridland, Valerie, and Kathryn Bartlett. 2006. Correctness, pleasantness, and degree of difference ratings across regions. *American Speech* 81.358–86.

Grootaers, Willem. 1959. Origin and nature of the subjective boundaries of dialects. *Orbis* 8.2.355–84.

Hartley, Laura C. 2005. The consequences of conflicting stereotypes: Bostonian perceptions of U.S. dialects. *American Speech* 80.4.388–405.

Hartley, Laura C., and Dennis R. Preston. 1999. The names of US English: Valley girl, cowboy, yankee, normal, nasal and ignorant. *Standard English: The widening debate,* ed. by Tony Bex and Richard J. Watts, 207–38. London: Routledge.

Hayakawa, S.I. 1978. *Language in thought and action,* 4th edition. New York: Harcourt Brace Jovanovich, Inc.

Irvine, Judith T., and Susan Gal. 2000. Language ideology and linguistic differentiation. Regimes of language: Ideologies, polities, and identities, ed. by Paul V. Kroskrity, 35–83. Santa Fe, NM: School of American Research Press.

James, William. 1907. *Pragmatism: A new name for some old ways of thinking.* New York: Longmans, Green, and Co.

Labov, William; Sharon Ash; and Charles Boberg. 2006. *The atlas of North American English: Phonetics, phonology and sound change, a multimedia reference tool.* Berlin: Mouton de Gruyter.

McGowan, Kevin B. 2015. Social expectation improves speech perception in noise. *Language and Speech* 58.4.502–21.

Niedzielski, Nancy, and Dennis R. Preston. 2000. *Folk linguistics.* Berlin: Mouton de Gruyter.

Preston, Dennis R. (1982). Perceptual dialectology: Mental maps of United States dialects from a Hawaiian perspective. *Working Papers in Linguistics* 14(2).5–49, ed. by D. Preston. (Special issue on language attitudes in Hawaii.) Honolulu, HI: Department of Linguistics, University of Hawaii at Manoa.

Preston, Dennis R. 1989. *Perceptual dialectology: Non-linguists' view of aerial linguistics.* Dordrecht: Foris.

Preston, Dennis R. 1993. The uses of folk linguistics. *International Journal of Applied Linguistics* 3.181–259.

Preston, Dennis R. 1996. Where the worst English is spoken. *Varieties of English around the World: Focus on the USA*, ed. by Edgar Schneider, 297–360. Amsterdam: John Benjamins.

Preston, Dennis R. 1997. The South: The touchstone. *Language variety in the South revisited*, ed. by C. Bernstein, T. Nunnally and R. Sabino, 311–51. Tuscaloosa, AL: The University of Alabama Press.

Preston, Dennis R. 1999. A language attitude approach to the perception of regional variety. *Handbook of perceptual dialectology*, vol. 1, ed. by D. R. Preston, 359–73. Amsterdam: John Benjamins.

Reed, John Shelton. 1993. *My tears spoiled my aim, and other reflections on Southern culture.* Columbia, MO: University of Missouri Press.

Sibata, Takesi. 1959. Consciousness of dialect boundaries. *Handbook of perceptual dialectology*, vol. 1, ed. by Dennis Preston, 39–62 (1999). Amsterdam: John Benjamins.

Smith, Grant W. 1998. The political impact of name sounds. *Communication Monographs* 65.154–72.

Tamasi, Susan. 2003. *Cognitive patterns of linguistic perceptions.* Athens, GA: University of Georgia dissertation.

5

LOCAL PLANETS

The view from home

Introduction

In this chapter, we continue to develop our understanding of nonlinguist views of speech by examining the labels given by respondents for their local areas. While previous chapters have shown that the macro-level perceptions of the US as a whole and the South in particular show a prevalence of relatively superficial stereotypes, this chapter explores how micro-level studies of dialect landscapes produce more nuanced descriptions of language, place, and identity, ultimately focusing on the concept of 'home'.

Here, we analyze and assess specific beliefs about the salience of 'local'. Most of the data that we explore comes from perceptual dialectology studies where respondents are asked to focus their attention on creating dialect boundaries within a single state. As discussed in Chapters 3 and 4, when we zoom closer into a more constricted area, the responses given by study participants show greater depth and gradation in the labels and categories that appear. We continue to see similar larger patterns that are now predictable in language attitude research – a focus on status, solidarity, and general geographic distinctions – however, looking at the divisions and comments included in individual participant maps reflects that attitudes towards linguistic variation are multifaceted, idiosyncratic, and nuanced. Of course, perceptual maps at a larger scale, such as a national map, often do show more detail (more lines, more descriptors) in the areas that are local and/or well known to respondents. Therefore, the idea that we would see complex maps at a local scale is not surprising.

In localized views, just as in macro-level studies, we see that binomial categories, ones that tend to pit entities against each other in a 'good vs. bad' dichotomy, continue to direct participant responses. Most meaningful seem to be divisions such as 'southern vs. northern', 'urban vs. rural', and 'city vs. country'. Crucially, labels and categories associated with solidarity and connectedness clearly emerge. Taken together and viewed with more detailed labels of local areas, we get a picture of one particular dichotomy – us vs. them – as a significant concept for nonlinguists. Included in this dichotomy is the recognition of one's place within a community and as a resident of a particular space.

As we have already seen in Chapters 3 and 4, linguistic perceptions of the South, including by Southerners themselves, are often contentious and contradictory, and reveal a strong, collective sense of linguistic insecurity (see also Preston 1996; Tamasi 2003; Cramer 2016). Therefore, it might seem that focusing on local language in the South, as our data analysis does, would reveal similar contradictions. While signs of linguistic insecurity do appear on state-level maps, we also see that negative views of the South are generally not applied to the places that are truly local for individual respondents. An analysis of the categories and labels that are used to describe speech in local areas reveals how Southerners reconcile negative beliefs about the South along with their positive views of home. They also reveal an even more complex belief planet.

In order to focus on perceptions of local speech, we must start with a discussion of PLACE itself. We approach the concept of local as subjective and place as phenomenological.

The nuances of place

While a plethora of research, including our own studies presented throughout this book, has made clear that language attitudes are regularly connected to geography or regionality, we can expand this further by moving beyond a reference to geography or even cartography to argue that nonlinguists' perceptions of language are more accurately described as being closely connected to the concept of place. Place, as a theoretical concept, has long been important to both traditional and perceptual approaches to dialectology. Within traditional dialect study, the emphasis has been on presenting phonological, grammatical, and lexical items as inherently connected to an objective and bounded physical entity. In this way, traditional dialectology ignores the 'socially rich' (Britain 2009:142) understanding of place as something more than 'a canvas onto which dialectological findings could be painted' (Britain 2009:144). While the earliest studies that aimed to map attitudes toward language variation, such as Weijnen (1946) and Sibata (1959, reprinted in Preston 1999), also focused solely on geography, further studies in perceptual dialectology quickly showed that there was more to nonlinguist perceptions than a simple connection between linguistic features (real or imagined) and geographic location. Thus, an expanded definition of 'place' is crucial for a comprehensive understanding of nonlinguist perceptions.

Here, we use the term 'place' as defined by humanistic geographers and explained in Johnstone's (2004) analysis of the role of place in sociolinguistic research. This view maintains that place is both physical and phenomenological, and it is socially constructed through the actions and attitudes of its residents.

Place is categorical; it includes geographic as well as social and experiential information. Therefore, this concept of place is subjective, and it diverges from the view of place as a reference solely to location (Johnstone 2004:66–67). This extended definition allows us to understand linguistic perceptions in greater depth, as part of a whole body of indexical points. When people associate language with place, they are linking speech not only with latitude and longitude, but with their views of the people and community that call that area home. Or, as Scollon and Scollon (2003:ix) write in the preface to *Discourses in Place*: 'Language indexes the world'. Thus, the link between the speech used in an area (or perceived to be used in that area) and the social traits associated with those speakers is inherent in the definition of place itself.

In eschewing the objective understanding of place in traditional dialectology, perceptual dialectology presents a view that connects nonlinguists' thoughts, beliefs, and attitudes about language to space beyond the sociopolitical and geographic facts within which their beliefs are enacted. Cramer and Montgomery (2016:xiii) say that perceptual dialectology, then, 'allows researchers to question assumptions often made about the close connections between place, language, and identity' and 'provides the right tools for understanding how place conditions non-linguists' thoughts about language'.

Geography acts as a reference point for all of the other, more abstract information involved in language attitudes. It is the hook upon which people can hang their perceptions. It is something that is readily understood, something that seems tangible. In fact, it is quite natural to reference the speech of a place. For example, there is a general recognition that there is indeed a place called Charleston and that the people who reside there not only actually speak to one another, but do so in patterned ways that index their residency. Perhaps a natural byproduct of the methodology, studies in perceptual dialectology show that the primary thing that nonlinguists access when discussing language variation is often geography or regionality. For example, Preston's (1989:69) early work was designed to showcase that language attitudes could, in fact, be linked to geographic entities, showing quantitatively that 'the ranking of respondents' perceptions of language correctness has areal significance'. Though especially true when participant responses are elicited through the use of a map, even in cases where such attitudes are elicited without a map (e.g. Tamasi 2003), geography continues to dominate the perceptions that are discovered. Even if one cannot give specific information about the linguistic features associated with or spoken in a particular place, they have a general idea of what the language of that place sounds like, or at least an idea of other locations that share this type of speech.

The concreteness of geography would make it seem that other types of information, such as assessments of pleasantness, correctness, trustworthiness, etc., are much more abstract and, thus, would seem to be less immediately accessible to nonlinguists. However, this is not the case, and decades of work in perceptual dialectology and language attitude studies have shown that social information is intimately connected to geography. A respondent from Massachusetts might not know exactly how a Charlestonian speaks, but they do know that it is different than a speaker from Boston. They might also know that a Charleston speaker sounds like someone drinking sweet tea on a front porch telling stories. Thus, ideas about language, or rather ideas about its speakers – sweet tea drinking, front porch sitting, and storytelling – are intimately wrapped up with location. This is what we mean by PLACE.

Nonlinguist perceptions of place show a highly complex interaction of both spatial and social information. As Joshua Fishman reminds us, language

> is not merely a *carrier* of content, whether latent or manifest. Language itself *is* content, a referent for loyalties and animosities, an indication of social statuses and personal relationships, a marker of situations and topics as well as of the societal goals and the large-scale value-laden arenas of interaction that typify every speech community.
>
> (1997:27, emphasis in original)

Examining nonlinguist responses in terms of place rather than geography reveals the saliency of the social information that is integrated into the concept of place. Crucially, it is this understanding of place as a set of social traits and goals that actually makes geography meaningful in linguistic attitudes. According to Reed (2020):

> As the investigation into the impact of place has developed and evolved, researchers have noted that it is not merely place itself that is the most important, rather the speaker's *relationship* to place that is perhaps the most crucial aspect.
>
> (1, emphasis in original)

People in different locations do speak differently from one another, and people do hear these differences, but it is the connection of language to place, with all of its complexities that the term brings, that is primary in folk linguistic views. Additionally, as we will see in the data below, this approach shows that beliefs about language and place are highly subjective and independently held.

Think globally, act locally

People love talking about local language. From jokes and memes that reference local varieties to dialect books, dictionaries, and tchotchkes sold online and at tourist attractions, folks like to see their local varieties represented. The index-ing of identity through language is so strong that most any public representation of a local identity will inevitably discuss language. For example, a quick Google search shows that the top results for 'Boston Memes' (Figure 5.1) specifically reference language variation and its salience to Boston identity (while also acting as a linguistic guide for those not already in the know). A more focused search

FIGURE 5.1 Top results for Google search 'Boston Memes', February 2, 2020.

of 'Boston language memes' brings up over 9.2 million results. Of course, this attention to and interest in local speech does not apply to only one area of the US.

The ubiquity of these pieces shows that people do, in fact, recognize the speech around them. Linguistic variation is salient in popular culture, as evidenced by those items mentioned above and by countless examples in television, film, and other media modalities that highlight the importance of linguistic variation for character development and story progression. Johnstone (2010:1) argues that this 'commodification of languages and varieties' is strong evidence of the amount of attention that is commonly paid to linguistic variation. While the potential exists for such representations of local speech to be used for devious and derogatory purposes (e.g. countless dialect memes angrily suggesting that there is a 'correct' term for a carbonated beverage in American English), they tend to be used to show the pride that people hold in being from a particular place.

As of January 2020, a search on Amazon.com for dialect books brings up, not one or two, but nine different books just on the linguistic varieties spoken in Pittsburgh. While some are written for a more academic audience, such as Johnstone et al.'s (2015) book *Pittsburgh Speech and Pittsburghese*, most are written for a non-academic audience by non-academics (e.g. *Pittsburghese from Ahrn to Yinz*, written by the staff of the Heinz History Center 2015). Regardless of audience, however, these books are not simply linguistic descriptions of a specific geographic dialect, but inherently include the multiplex social and linguistic information of place. As Johnstone (2004) explains:

> Pittsburghese is a set of linguistic features that overlaps with but is not the same as the set a sociolinguist might choose on the basis of observation. It is also a set of ideas about what those features mean, a local folk discourse about variation.
>
> (78)

The perception of Pittsburghese as a distinct language variety is not based on linguistic features that are exclusive to the Pittsburgh area. Features found in and around Pittsburgh can also be found throughout Appalachia, but these features

FIGURE 5.2 'Bless Your Heart' dialect button from the North Carolina Language & Life Project. Source: Jennifer Cramer.

have social meaning for those who live in Pittsburgh as being representative of this place. The use of these features, such as *yinz* for the second person plural pronoun or the monophthongization of [aw] in words like *downtown*, is meaningful in that it represents a communal identity. Their use signifies that the speaker identifies with, and is generally proud of calling Pittsburgh 'home'.

Similarly, in the South, public and personal displays of words and phrases evoke not only the connotation of the words displayed, but also – and, one could argue, primarily – images of the South and feelings of connectedness to this special place and its people. The sought-after items in Figures 5.2 and 5.3 are

FIGURE 5.3 'All Y'all' T-shirt sold by the Bitter Southerner. Source: Susan Tamasi.

worn to display pride in the South and Southernness. Multi-media sites like 'The Bitter Southerner', 'It's a Southern Thing', and 'WellRed Comedy', which bring together humor, storytelling, history, and stereotype, are able to boast several million followers. Wolfram and Reaser's *Talkin' Tar Heel: How Our Voices Tell the Story of North Carolina* (2014) has sold over 7,500 copies.

Perceptions of local in the South

Typically, for our respondents, views of Southern vs. non-Southern affect distinctions in large-scale (national and regional) maps (see Chapters 3 and 4). The salient distinction between Southern and non-Southern highlights that it is the concept of Southernness that is primary for respondents. They distinguish areas by determining conceptually what is the South and what isn't the South, as opposed to categorizing South vs. North (or South vs. West, etc.), which focuses on cardinal direction and places both locations as perceptually equivalent.

Even with very individualized views of where people speak similarly and differently from one another, Georgia participant responses show a pattern of a cohesive Southern dialect region that stands out clearly from the rest of the country. Figures 5.4 and 5.5 are just two examples of how a Southern dialect region is seen and distinguished by Georgia respondents. (In each map, different shading represents a different dialect group.) In each case, the majority of the

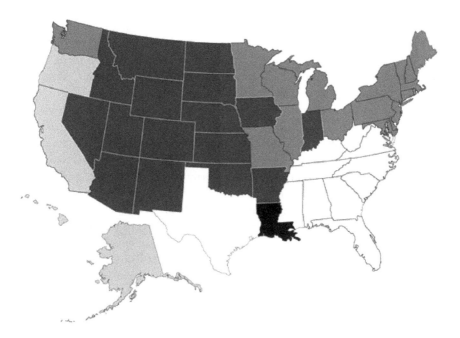

FIGURE 5.4 A perceptual map from a Georgia respondent.

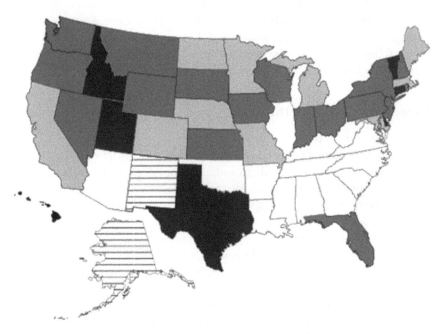

FIGURE 5.5 Another Georgia respondent perceptual map.

states in the Southeast, including those considered the Southern Trough (Gould & White 1986), are placed together as a singular dialect region. Specifically, both respondents are in agreement that a Southern speech region is made up by Georgia, Alabama, Mississippi, Tennessee, Kentucky, West Virginia, Virginia, North Carolina, and South Carolina.

However, this prevalent view of a larger, cohesive South is primarily displayed only when we examine perceptions using a national-scale map. At a smaller scale, the South is often broken down into smaller speech areas, or subregions. Thus, when we zoom in to the perceptions of speech within individual states, we see an even more nuanced picture. And an analysis of the labels used at this level reveals additional factors that are salient for determining what is and is not local. This analysis will be the focus of our discussion below.

When examining smaller-scale maps, including those of one state only, the data show a conceptualization of speech that is connected not simply to geography but to the social construction of the community in that location, i.e. place. For many respondents across the US, the differentiation between city and country, or urban and rural, is a significant factor in linguistic perceptions of local places (e.g. Hartley 2005; Evans 2011; Carmichael 2016).

Figure 5.6 shows such a map, in which, for this Kentucky respondent, most significant for her delineation of speech areas are the labels 'city', 'country', and a 'mix' of the two. Note that, for the respondent, the actual city does not matter

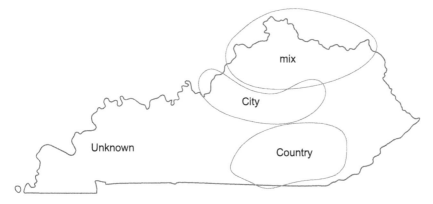

FIGURE 5.6 Map drawn by a 21-year-old female respondent from Lexington, Kentucky.

(though it approximates the region encompassing both Louisville and Lexington, the state's two largest cities), but it is the distinction between city and country, and the contrast with spaces that are neither city nor country, that is salient. It is less about identifying with or feeling a close connection to the cities of Louisville and Lexington, and more of a connection to a generic city-space, which is unlike what we saw in the discussion above concerning Pittsburgh, where an identity based on living in or being from the city of Pittsburgh is primary. Furthermore, in her map, the respondent claims to not know about the speech in the western part of the state, likely because it does not fit clearly within the city vs. country categorization that guides the other choices.

Respondent labels, in order to make the distinction clearer, will sometimes move beyond a dichotomous categorization of urban vs. rural, and produce a more distinct conceptualization of the local. In Figure 5.7, a Kentucky respondent uses the labels 'non-country', 'semi country', 'very country', as well as just 'country'. Thus, at the local level, the city vs. country distinction is still salient, as it was at the national and regional levels, but in a multiplex view of the state, especially given specific geopolitical facts about Kentucky's population, distribution of population, and land use, a straight binomial division between city and country is not enough to show a complete picture of perceived language use. For nonlinguists, there needs to be a salient category in which to connect their linguistic divisions, but when looking at a local area, an area that they view in complex ways, then they often need more than a simple two-way distinction to show the different subregions. In fact, Cramer (2016) found that for her Kentucky respondents it was the tripart distinction between urban, rural, and mountain rural that was significant.

Responses of 'not sure', 'I don't know', or 'unknown' are equally salient in nonlinguist perceptions. As seen in Figures 5.6, 5.7, and 5.8, these labels are

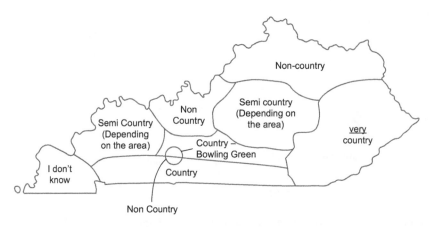

FIGURE 5.7 Map drawn by an 18-year-old female respondent from Richmond, Kentucky.

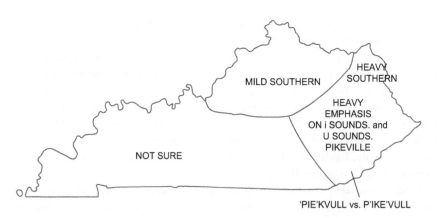

FIGURE 5.8 Map drawn by a 32-year-old male respondent from Lexington, Kentucky.

regularly used on respondent maps. In perceptual dialectology, these types of labels can show that this is an area completely unknown to the respondent, but more likely, they reveal that the geographic space is not connected to a signifi-cant category, such as 'country' or 'city' or 'Southern', as we find in other areas on these maps. For example, the place marked on the map in Figure 5.8 as 'not sure' does not index for the respondent this salient category of 'Southern' (or its sub-categories of 'mild Southern' or 'heavy Southern'). It does not fit neatly in with the respondent's schema for perceptions of speech in Kentucky. In other words, it did not activate a part of his belief planet that has a direct connection to local speech. It is not likely that the respondent knows nothing about this region; in fact, by labeling it at all, he shows that he is aware that there may be something worth noting. Perhaps he is familiar with cultural locales like the Corvette Museum and Mammoth Cave, both of which are located in this geographic space. Or maybe he knows of the culinary treats, like barbecue in Paducah and Owensboro. But he has nothing to say about the language there, meaning he cannot lump it in with the others indicated, but rather, that language does not stand out as an important feature of the place.

Additionally, Figure 5.8 shows that once the primary markers of 'Southern' are applied to particular places within the state, then respondents are able to access – when available to them as a part of their belief planets – additional information about individual areas. Here, we see a phonological representation of the local speech. Eastern Kentucky is not just 'Heavy Southern' but is distinct from the other labels of Southern in the state due to speakers' 'heavy emphasis on i sounds and u sounds'.

Local identities: us vs. them

As noted in previous chapters, our Southern respondents are fully aware of the negative attitudes and stereotypes that are prevalent around Southern speech. And we recognize that speakers often internalize these views, leading to linguistic insecurity. However, perceptual dialectology and language attitude research from the very beginning (cf. Lambert 1967; Preston 1989) concluded that speakers who rate their own speech low according to status traits usually rate themselves high for traits related to solidarity. This tendency results in the 'stupid but friendly' dichotomy commonly attached to Southern speech that is well-known to Southerners. Therefore, even in the face of negative attitudes, speakers of stigmatized forms tend to still show pride in where they are from.

Additionally, we have seen that 'Southern' is one of the most commonly used labels in perceptual dialectology research at all map levels. For national-level maps, this separates the South from the non-South, and for regional-level maps, it reveals subregions within the target area (see Chapters 3 and 4). For Southerners giving their perceptions about state- and local-level speech, the use of the label 'Southern' can do many things. First, it can show a geographic division of the state itself, and is usually seen with other cardinal labels, as we see in Figure 5.9. Second, it can represent a recognition of the area as a part of the South and acts as a statement about Southern identity. Third, it can distinguish between a conceptualized 'us' versus 'them' within the local area, with 'them' often representing a recognition of the negative stigma towards the South. (See Figure 5.10.) This last point is usually represented in statements such as: I'm Southern but not *that* type of Southern.

Qualitative data from perceptual studies and sociolinguistic interviews also support the view that Southerners will make a distinction within the South between 'us' and 'them', allowing for both feelings of pride in their Southern identity as well as agreement with the stigma surrounding Southern speech. For example, in their work in Roswell, GA, Kretzschmar et al. (n.d.) found

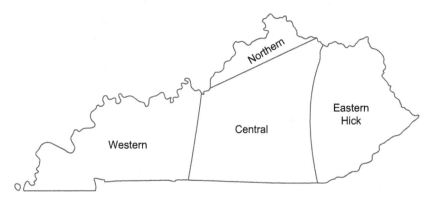

FIGURE 5.9   Map drawn by a 21-year-old male respondent from Lexington, Kentucky.

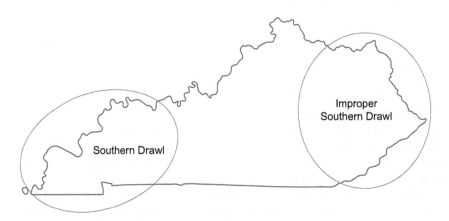

FIGURE 5.10   Map drawn by a 23-year-old female respondent from Louisville, Kentucky.

comments like: 'he's a good ol' Southern boy, um, but he's very well educated … and you can tell … but he's, he's, he still has the Southernness', where a noted pause reflects a disconnect between the constructs of educated and Southern. Additionally, used as a type of stand-in for negative connotations of Southern, four of the suburban Roswell respondents used the term 'country' (a total of 14 times) in reference to speech in Georgia, but specified that the label did not apply to themselves.

In Tamasi (2003), in both the pile sort data and the qualitative interviews that accompanied them, we also see this 'us vs. them' dichotomy applied within the South, and toward Georgia in particular. The only statistically significant categorizations for any of the 50 states were descriptions of Georgia as attractive, honest, friendly, nice, pleasant, and trustworthy – but also incorrect, lazy, and unintelligent. Many of the Georgia respondents who lived in more urban or suburban areas said they recognized the existence of a Southern accent, but that they themselves did not have it, and that for those who did, 'friendly but stupid' applied. Therefore, these 'other' Southerners – those who sounded stereotypically Southern – were good people, but were not folks that the respondents identified closely with. This distancing allows respondents to recognize the stigmatized perceptions of the speech of the local area without having it apply directly to them.

A negative assessment of the speech in the South can be balanced not only by a contrast in status vs. solidarity (i.e. 'stupid but friendly') but also by positive views of a more localized area, often equated to where the respondent is from or to culturally prestigious cities. For example, Tamasi (2003) found differences in the linguistic perceptions of Georgians who identified with a greater 'South' versus those who identified with a more limited area, such as a particular city or town. Several of her respondents said that they themselves were from Atlanta or its suburbs and therefore did not use the speech that they perceived as being used in the rest of the state. They also often referenced their pride in NOT sounding like the rest of the South. Cramer (2013) found similar results in her Kentucky data. Several respondents who overtly and explicitly linked the South with concepts like plantations and Southern belles, specifically disconnected these stereotyped perceptions from cities like Louisville or Lexington. Even though they claim other aspects of Southern identity connected with these cities, traits such as friendliness, a connection to family, and a love for the Kentucky Derby, the lack of association with plantations, Southern belles, and the like keep these cities from being a part of a 'real' South. As such, these respondents create a wall that separates these places from a larger, stigmatized South.

The data from Kentucky also show how respondents divide states into more localized areas to highlight areas that they more closely identify with. In Figure 5.11, the respondent not only marks city in contrast to country but

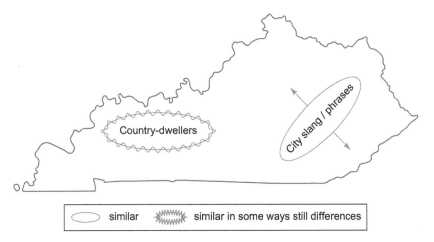

FIGURE 5.11 Map drawn by a 21-year-old female respondent from Louisville, Kentucky.

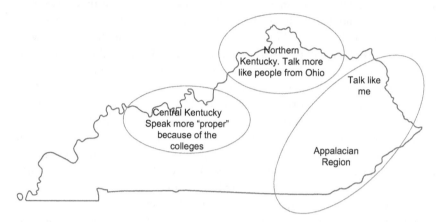

FIGURE 5.12 Map drawn by a 21-year-old female respondent from Sandy Hook, Kentucky.

notes which areas are 'similar' and those which are 'similar in some ways' but where there are 'still differences'. Kentucky is a place that she identifies with, but she does not identify with the entire state equally; there are perceived differences in speech that keep them separate. In Figure 5.12, we see even more divisions perceived between areas within Kentucky, including a close identification with the 'Appalacian Region' where they 'Talk like me' versus those in northern Kentucky who 'Talk more like people from Ohio' and those in Central Kentucky who 'Speak more "proper" because of the colleges'. Here, the respondent uses her own local speech and identity (Appalachian) as a point of comparison for the other perceived areas. Kentucky is home, but the respondent does not identify her speech as being from just anywhere in the state.

Individuality of responses

In our investigation of national and regional views of linguistic perceptions, we concentrated on the beliefs that were shared across groups of respondents. However, examining perceptions at a local scale readily reveals that beliefs at this level tend to be more independent, idiosyncratic, and reflective of the experiences and beliefs of the individual. The more local the focus, the more distinctive the responses. In our respective studies, we have seen hundreds, if not thousands, of individual maps, and no two look exactly the same. They may follow larger patterns about where dialect regions are believed to exist or that labels fall into categories of status vs. solidarity or us vs. them. But as the map base zooms in to local areas, responses – from the number and location of areas defined to the different descriptors used – differ extensively.

For us, the fact that there is no simple pattern to these perceptions makes them truly fascinating. They show that nonlinguists draw from similar types of

information in order to describe and reflect on areas of perceived linguistic differences, but the specific information that is included in these views are discrete
and individualized. People do categorize and index thoughts about language, but
how that happens is unique. The sheer amount of individualized data can at first
seem disorganized, if not chaotic. However, a closer examination shows that,
when taken within the context of planets of belief – i.e. by looking at every map
as being a snapshot of the individual's own belief planet – we find clarity in the
chaos. In the maps above (5.6–5.12), we see that while one person might focus
their perceptions on concepts of the South (e.g. Southern, heavy Southern, or
improper Southern) another might focus on levels of country-ness (e.g. country,
semi-country, or very country). While not everyone has a singular focus that
guides all decisions in their maps – and in fact, most maps show a combination
of information that people associate with linguistic variation – patterns tend to
emerge for each respondent. Importantly, visions of local speech areas reveal the
depth and complexity of an individual's perceptions.

Respondents generally give more information when talking about areas that
are local to them. This is regularly interpreted as a reflection of their simply
knowing more about the areas that they have more experience with. Similarly,
they might also say more about areas that they frequently visit or that their family is from. Even larger-level maps often contain more detail about the areas that
are local to the respondents. Additionally, the amount of detail given wanes for
areas the further they are away from where the person lives. Thus, it appears that
proximity (e.g. Montgomery 2012) is a key factor in the development and depth
of perceptions. However, we argue that it is actually one's understanding of a
place – not experience with a location but the connection of geographic location
AND all of the social and personal information attached to it – that informs our
beliefs. This also might include linguistic information, such as specific words or
even stereotyped pronunciations, which are tied together with geography and
social categories in a belief planet. In fact, we can see this clearly for areas where
the language is stigmatized, such as the South, where geographic proximity of
the respondent is trumped by the strength of the belief planet.

The map in Figure 5.13 shows how a combination of different types of information can work together to present a complete picture of the respondent's view
of her home state. The cardinal directions are marked, showing a meaningful
(to her) distinction between these four points of the map. There are also city
labels to orient the map to where she has lived (see Nicholasville, Lex[ington],
Lou[isville], all marked with asterisks). Not only does she write 'Mountain' to
demarcate the Appalachian Mountains, but she actually draws a small mountain
ridge as well. However, even though these geographic points are notable and
obviously meaningful, in each case she has also included social and/or linguistic
information directly with the geographic. Thus, in the West, there are hicks. In
the East, there are hillbillies who say 'Get-r-done'. In the South, they say 'y'all'
and speak with a 'slow draw[l]'. Finally, in the central area, where she has lived,
this is where one can find a 'more general, Proper English' spoken. For this

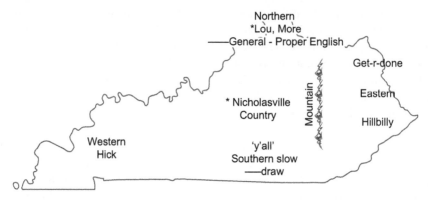

FIGURE 5.13 Map drawn by a 60-year-old female respondent from Taylorsville, Kentucky.

respondent, it is a combination of this information that is the foundation of her perceptions. And it is this information that is reflective of and supported by her belief planet.

Figure 5.14 similarly shows a mixture of information that makes up this respondent's mental maps. Again, we see combinations of geography (Mountain, Western), and linguistic or pseudo-linguistic information (twang, paced, quicker, slow, thick, Standard American English Dialect), and social views (Southern belle-esk, refined). This combination reveals that the respondent's belief planet connects multiple categories of information that are significantly and meaningfully related to one another. By comparing Figure 5.14 with Figure 5.13,

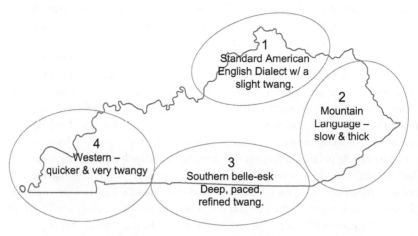

FIGURE 5.14 Map drawn by an 18-year-old female respondent from Lexington, Kentucky.

we note the appearance of the same larger categories – geography, social traits, linguistic features. However, the information included in these categories, or how they are specifically articulated, differ. For example, both respondents pull from a category of linguistic-type information in drawing their maps; however, they do so differently from one another. The respondent whose map is seen in Figure 5.13 uses 'draw[l]', 'y'all', and 'proper English', while the participant who drew Figure 5.14 includes as examples of linguistic information 'twangy', 'Standard American English', and 'Mountain language – slow and thick'.

Another key aspect regarding the individualism of perceptual maps is the sheer amount of information that is or is not included by a particular respondent. Whether it be the number of regions created or the number of descriptors used, the individuality of participant responses clearly reveals the complexity of nonlinguist perceptions toward speech. For example, Figures 5.15 and 5.16 show a tremendous amount of detail, while Figures 5.17 and 5.18 have hardly anything written on them.

An analysis of the variation in the number of comments given can give us insight into the complexity of the respondent's belief planet that serves as a base for these views. However, this does not mean that maps with limited information show that the respondent does not have any opinions about that area. It might be that their belief planets are less robust for this particular area; alternatively, it could mean the opposite – their belief planets for the area are so robust that they feel that reference to only a small portion of the information that they connect to that area is enough for anyone to access additional information, assuming that others share similar belief planets. Of course, it can also be the case that respondents are merely hesitant to include information that reveals their negative opinions towards others. While carrying out research in perceptual dialectology, it is not uncommon for researchers to hear comments from respondents such as 'Don't judge me' or 'I don't want to sound mean' or 'I can't write that down' when labeling areas that they view negatively. In fact, Tamasi found a notable,

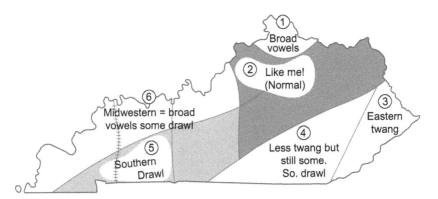

FIGURE 5.15 Map drawn by a 55-year-old female respondent from Lexington, Kentucky.

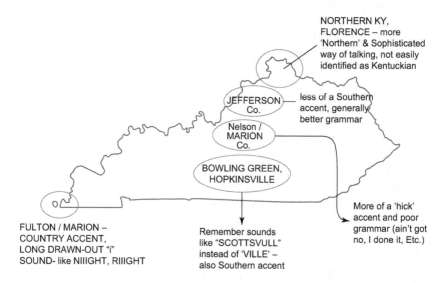

FIGURE 5.16 Map drawn by a 50-year-old female respondent from Bardstown, Kentucky.

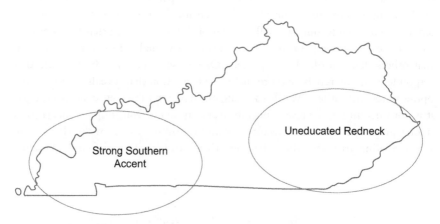

FIGURE 5.17 Map drawn by a 50-year-old female respondent from Louisville, Kentucky.

although not significant, difference in the number of negative associations given to speech areas when conducting research in the US shortly after the terrorist attacks in New York City on 9/11. Her respondents did not want to say anything disparaging about other Americans. (However, they were still okay with saying Southern speech sounded uneducated.)

At the end of the spectrum of more versus fewer comments, Figures 5.19 and 5.20 each have only one area circled with only one short descriptor. For the

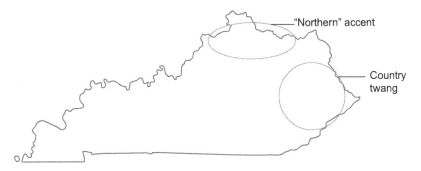

FIGURE 5.18 Map drawn by a 20-year-old female respondent from Scott County, Kentucky.

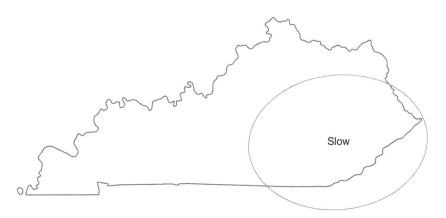

FIGURE 5.19 Map drawn by a 25-year-old male respondent from Bardstown, Kentucky.

map shown in Figure 5.19, all that the respondent felt he needed to complete the task and display his perceptions is one simple word, 'slow'. It might appear that this respondent simply did not want to put the time and energy into taking the survey, which could be true, but if that were the case, he would have taken even less time by writing nothing. Instead, he used a single term to get across his main view. Similarly, the respondent who produced Figure 5.20 also circled one area on the map, distinguishing the area where the hillbillies live from the rest of the state. Again, we can read this response as just the right amount of information for this respondent to depict the linguistic differences he perceives to exist in Kentucky. Each of these maps show independence in responses and highlights that information combines in unique ways in individuals' belief planets.

One of the strongest factors that lead to these individual differences in perceptions is personal experience. For example, with regard to region, whether the

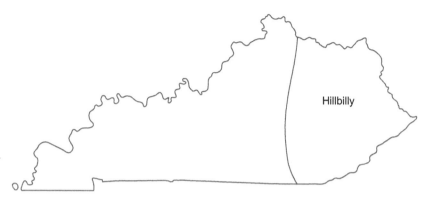

FIGURE 5.20 Map drawn by a 55-year-old male respondent from Versailles, Kentucky.

area is local or not local depends on who is doing the hearing or the experiencing, i.e. an egocentric view. Additionally, whether respondents are linguistically secure or insecure will affect their judgments of 'good' or 'bad' language (e.g. Preston 1989). Perceptions from person to person might be determined by the same categories, such as region, social acceptability, or even actual language features, but one's experiences with a place or a set of speakers can skew perceptions in different directions or emphasize different details, as we saw above. Even some of the earliest work on language attitudes highlighted the significance of respondent experience and identity. According to Lambert (1967:100):

> The type and strength of impression depends on characteristics of the speakers – their sex, age, the dialect they use, and, very likely, the social-class background as this is revealed in speech style. The impression also seems to depend on characteristics of the audience of *judges* – their age, sex, socio-economic background, their bilinguality and their own speech style.

Going back to the example we presented in Chapter 1, the smell of jasmine might conjure up memories of grandma's house for one person. However, for someone else, the smell of jasmine might remind them of the perfume of a lost love. Or it could simply bring to mind thoughts of flowers in general. In other words, these memories might be positive or negative depending on who is smelling the jasmine and what their personal experiences are. For different people, a different set of perceptions and therefore a different set of beliefs will be activated and accessed. Applied to language, the sound of Southern speech might bring back memories of a happy childhood for some, while for others, it might be a reminder of a particularly disliked individual, such as a bad co-worker or a corrupt public figure. Any linguistic feature that the hearer associates with Southern speech can trigger a whole set of memories and beliefs. Hearing someone say 'y'all' – or perhaps just being asked to fill out some strange linguistics survey about speech differences – can activate positive or negative reactions (or both) based on the individual's personal experiences.

Additionally, as people's experiences change across their lifespan, their perceptions and attitudes develop as well. As Reed (2018) points out, a speaker's relationship to place is not static, but dynamic. People may move to a different city or state; they might move back to a place that they only recognized as home after they had been gone for a time. Home might be where they grew up or where they finally settled down. As such, it would be interesting to examine a person's linguistic perceptions at various points in their life in order to track how personal experience and a changing understanding of 'place' and 'home' affect linguistic perceptions. While these experiences bring new information and understanding to a person's belief planets, we expect, due to their rather rigid nature, that firmly held beliefs, those instantiated from an early age and nurtured in early experiences, will remain, even in light of newly acquired components of the system as a whole.

Local planets

In this chapter, we have examined the perceptions that our Southern respondents have towards their local areas, showing how micro-level analyses reveal complex interactions of language, experience, identity, and place. While contradictory views of a 'friendly but stupid' sounding South still hold, respondents maintain their hold on a Southern identity while also distinguishing themselves from a stigmatized South. They use subregions, or hyper-localized areas, as ways of distinguishing 'us' from 'them' in order to maneuver the complexity and contradictions in their views of the South. To further accomplish this, their planets of belief connect multiplex networks of information, giving a singular belief planet the ability to find structure in seemingly chaotic sets of information.

While a national-level map shows the common perception of a cohesive Southern dialect area, usually revolving around the Southern Trough of the southeastern United States, our respondents continued to further divide individual states into subregions or subdialects of a larger South. Since studies at varying levels of scale show that at any base level, areas are divided further into smaller dialect areas, this is perhaps not surprising. However, for our Southern respondents, this division allows them to hold onto a Southern identity, while separating areas of closer versus more distant associations. This also shows that nonlinguists can recognize variation in language structure or use, even if they cannot describe these differences accurately.

We started this chapter with a discussion of place, and the analyses presented here support the view that when it comes to the local, it is the view of place – as a phenomenological construct that is made up of much more than geographic location – that is fundamental in understanding nonlinguists' perceptions. The metaphor of planets of belief helps us conceptualize these networks of information that people relate to place and allows us to see how this information attaches to language. Thus, we have seen geographic, linguistic, social, and categorical information bundled together. Additionally, for an individual, these bundles are further filtered through personal experience.

Looking back at the two maps of Kentucky that we saw in Figures 5.13 and 5.14 above, we noted that the labels that were used fell into the same categories, such as geography, social traits, and linguistic features. Thus, the belief planets of two different respondents, taken at a macro level, might look very much the same, for example the image presented in Figure 5.21. In fact, from a macro view, this singular image can actually represent the belief planets of several of our respondents.

However, when we zoom into a micro-level view of the belief planet of just one of the respondents, we see more detail underlying these categories. Figure 5.22 shows that the category of geography includes the concepts of Mountain, Western, and Southern, but it also shows that these concepts are also intimately connected to additional social and linguistic concepts. In fact, some of the respondent's labels themselves reveal these connections in that she provides phrases, such as 'Mountain language', 'Western – quicker and very twangy', that include an overlap of this information. We can compare this belief planet with the one represented in Figure 5.23, which also includes 'Mountain' and 'Western' in her geographic category. However, for this respondent, the West is where the 'hicks' live, not (necessarily) where the language is 'quicker and very twangy', and the Mountains are where people say 'Get-r-done'. Thus, a shared pattern of categories becomes much more individualized when we zoom into a micro level of individual belief planets.

These visual representations of belief planets as understood by considering two individual hand-drawn maps reveal the true nature of the planets of belief metaphor. Linguists, especially those from the Bloomfieldian structuralist paradigm, have long bemoaned the collection, use, and analysis of nonlinguist

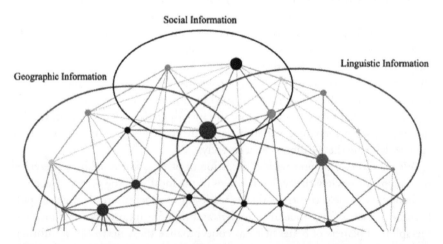

FIGURE 5.21 A belief planet at the macro level.

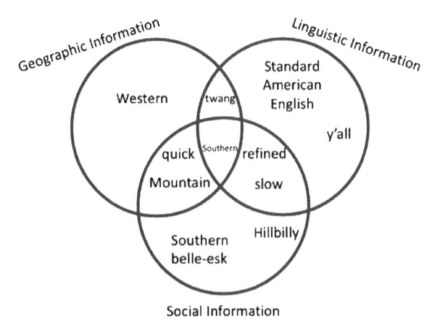

FIGURE 5.22   A belief planet at the micro level.

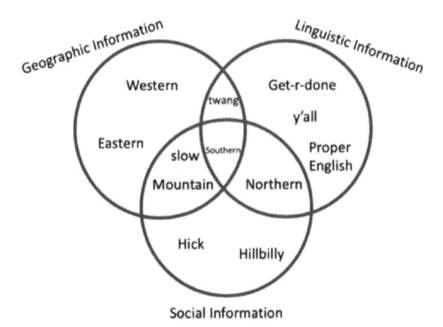

FIGURE 5.23   Another micro-level belief planet.

attitudes in linguistic research, not only because they were seen as secondary to production data itself but also because it was assumed that

> our culture maintains a loosely organized but fairly uniform system of pronouncements about language. Deviant speech forms in dialects other than the standard dialect are described as corruptions of the standard form ('mistakes', 'bad grammar') or branded as entirely out of bounds, on a par with the solecisms of a foreign speaker ('not English'). The forms of the standard dialect are justified on grounds of 'logic'.
>
> (Bloomfield 1944:45)

If believed, this statement renders any exploration of attitudes about language null and void from the start. Yet, as we see in these planet structures, the 'loosely organized' component of the statement is maintained; nevertheless, the variations seen here and elsewhere in perceptual dialectology research suggest that the system is not as uniform as one might be led to believe. The messy, individualistic data presented here and in countless other studies reveals that these kinds of beliefs are not only worthy of exploration but also fuel the study of other forms of variation that might be of interest in the study of language. Perceptual work at these local levels allows a real understanding of the on-the-ground categories used to describe linguistic variation in these geographic spaces and provides insight into the role of place as theorized here in those categorizations.

References

Bloomfield, Leonard. 1944. Secondary and tertiary responses to language. *Language* 20.45–55.

Britain, David. 2009. Language and space: The variationist approach. *Language and space: An international handbook of linguistic variation*, ed. by Peter Auer and Jürgen Erich Schmidt, 142–62. Berlin: Mouton de Gruyter.

Carmichael, Katie. 2016. Place-linked expectations and listener awareness of regional accents. *Awareness and control in sociolinguistic research*, ed. by A. M. Babel, 152–76. Cambridge: Cambridge University Press.

Cramer, Jennifer. 2013. Styles, stereotypes, and the South: Constructing identities at the linguistic border. *American Speech* 88.2.144–67.

Cramer, Jennifer. 2016. *Contested Southernness: The linguistic production and perception of identities in the borderlands*. Publication of the American Dialect Society 100. Durham, NC: Duke University Press.

Cramer, Jennifer, and Chris Montgomery. 2016. *Cityscapes and perceptual dialectology: Global perspectives on non-linguists' knowledge of the dialect landscape*. Language and Social Life 5. Berlin: Mouton de Gruyter.

Evans, Betsy. 2011. "Seattletonian" to "Faux Hick": Perceptions of English in Washington state. *American Speech* 86.4.383–414.

Fishman, Joshua A. 1997. The sociology of language. *Sociolinguistics. Modern linguistics series*, ed. by Nikolas Coupland and Adam Jaworski, 25–30. London: Palgrave.

Gould, Peter, and Rodney White. 1986. *Mental maps*, 2nd edition. Boston, MA: Allen & Unwin.

Hartley, Laura C. 2005. The consequences of conflicting stereotypes: Bostonian perceptions of U.S. dialects. *American Speech* 80.4.388–405.

Heinz History Center. 2015. *Pittsburghese from ahrn to yinz*. Pittsburgh, PA: Senator John Heinz History Center.

Johnstone, Barbara. 2004. Place, globalization, and linguistic variation. *Sociolinguistic variation: Critical reflections*, ed. by C. Fought, 65–83. New York: Oxford University Press.

Johnstone, Barbara. 2010. Indexing the local. *Handbook of language and globalization*, ed. by N. Coupland, 386–405. Oxford: Wiley-Blackwell.

Johnstone, Barbara; Daniel Baumgardt; Maeve Eberhardt; and Scott Kiesling. 2015. *Pittsburgh speech and Pittsburghese*. Berlin /Boston: Mouton De Gruyter.

Kretzschmar, William A., Jr.; Becky Childs; Bridget Anderson; and Sonja Lanehart. n.d. *Roswell voices project*. http://www.lap.uga.edu/Projects/ROSWELL/.

Lambert, Wallace E. 1967. A social psychology of bilingualism. *Journal of Social Issues* 23.91–109.

Montgomery, Chris. 2012. The effect of proximity in perceptual dialectology. *Journal of Sociolinguistics* 16.5.638–68.

Preston, Dennis R. 1989. Preston, Dennis R. 1996. Where the worst English is spoken. *Focus on the USA*, ed. by Edgar Schneider, 297–360. Amsterdam: John Benjamins.

Reed, Paul E. 2018. The importance of Appalachian identity: A case study in rootedness. *American Speech* 93.3–4.409–24.

Reed, Paul E. 2020. Place and language: Links between speech, region, and connection to place. *WIREs Cognitive Science* e1524.1–11.

Sibata, Takesi. 1959. Consciousness of dialect boundaries. Reprinted in Dennis R. Preston (1999), 39–62.

Scollon, Ron, and Suzie Wong Scollon. 2003. *Discourses in place*. New York: Routledge.

Tamasi, Susan. 2003. *Cognitive patterns of linguistic perceptions*. Athens, GA: University of Georgia dissertation.

Weijnen, Antonius A. 1946. De grenzen tussen de Oost-Noordbrabantse dialecten onderling [The borders between the dialects of eastern North Brabant]. *Oost-Noordbrabantse dialectproblemen* [Eastern North Brabant dialect problems], ed. by A. A. Weijnen, J. M. Renders, and J. van Ginneken. Bijdragen en Mededelingen der Dialectencommissie van de Koninklijke Nederlandse Akademie van Wetenschappen te Amsterdam 8.1–15.

Wolfram, Walt, and Jeffrey Reaser. 2014. *Talkin' tar heel: How our voices tell the story of North Carolina*. Chapel Hill, NC: University of North Carolina Press.

6

MAKING SENSE OF OUR PLANETS

Introduction

In this final chapter, we reexamine the concept of linguistic planets of belief in light of the data presented in the previous chapters. We hope to have shown that while there are patterns to our linguistic beliefs, we also find ourselves enveloped in idiosyncratic understandings of the nature of language structure and use. The patterns we do find reveal a high level of solidity among perceivers of language in the United States.

The chapter takes a look at how the different levels of perception that we examined (national, regional, and local) show both similarities and differences, within and across map and participant types. We evaluate what these differences mean for understanding not only variation in perception but also variation in production. As the previous chapters explored both positive and negative beliefs, we use this chapter as a way to suggest that the words we use, like the labels we give to describe someone's language, can have an impact on a person's own self-worth. We explicitly encourage readers to carefully consider the negative perceptions they carry about people and their linguistic varieties, with a goal of helping people understand how language works and the ways in which certain beliefs about language are based in a poor understanding of the nuance of language.

Turning to our own results, the combination of these various studies, all conducted in, around, and about the American South, can help elucidate the complicated nature of variation in American English.

Comparing levels of scale

When we described the results of studies performed on the national-scale maps, the image of perceptions of American English was not very detailed or nuanced.

In study after study, we have seen that the most prominent region perceived is the American South, with the North coming in close second. While the rest of country received some recognition, the North–South dichotomy loomed large in the minds of these American dialect perceivers. Planet USA, as exemplified in the perceptions given by respondents from Tennessee, accentuates this North/South divide, giving secondary consideration to the California variety (see Figure 3.36), but always maintaining the importance of Northernness and Southernness for Tennesseans. In Planet USA, there are vast gaps in awareness, perceptions, and beliefs concerning the majority of the country in between California and Tennessee. In Chapter 3 we claimed that this might be a result of a lack of alignment between the cartographic map the respondents wrote on and the cognitive map they have constructed in their minds throughout their lives. But as we saw in Chapters 4 and 5, some Southerners fully ascribe to this adage: 'if you can't say something nice, don't say anything at all'. In those cases, leaving the vast majority of the country unlabeled could mean either they have nothing to say or they have nothing nice to say. Lack of information necessarily leaves us with a lack of answers. But if other kinds of data can be presented, we may have some further clues about those belief planets.

For example, if we further examine the patterns in the data with respect to national-level perceptions, it is not surprising to see that respondents often use the broad stereotypes most commonly associated with regions they point to in order to provide some detail about places with which they are at least remotely familiar. They know that Southerners are stereotyped as 'slow' speakers and that Californians are all 'surfer dudes'. There are country people everywhere, and the few areas that are worth considering as separate in the whole country are often Louisiana and Texas, thanks to the stereotypes about their specific accents and identities, and how they are differentiated from other (Southern) American ones. For example, what we encounter often said about Texas is that it is its own thing – the state that sees itself as separate from the rest of the US – as opposed to hearing perceptions specifically about speech. The larger stereotypes seem to guide participants in constructing the dialect landscapes at the largest scale, which, given the size of the country and the wide variation exhibited in everything (e.g. foods, clothing, popular culture), is perhaps not surprising. Thus, the planet of belief that emerges at this highest level is made up from common stereotypes and does not show much nuance, even in the description of the region the respondents call home.

Because of this overreliance on stereotypes at the national level, few details were provided in the most frequent descriptions of the South. When we looked at the tail of an A-curve (see Figure 3.29) for the one-time occurrences of labels, for example, there did not appear to be a regular pattern in it either. What information was given tended to focus on the people and the geography, with only a small bit of information regarding speech. Similarly, when participants described the North, specific areas like New York, New Jersey, New England, Boston, and Michigan show up as quintessential members and the speech is described as proper, fast, or slang. But, again, there was not much detail provided. Yet the North–South dichotomy is maintained. This, too, is a broad American stereotype, but what their preservation of the distinction tells us about their belief planets is that this stereotype is most prominent for the participants drawing the maps. It is part of what they know about their dialect landscape – that Northerners are different than Southerners – and, from a perceptual dialectology perspective, it is this kind of information that people rely on when attempting to solve the communicative problems they encounter in their day-to-day lives.

It is crucial to note the role of the map itself as a possible cause for such surface treatment; as we saw in Chapters 4 and 5, the more we zoomed into smaller, more local regions that the respondents are invested in, the more complex and nuanced the perceptions were. While the zoomed-out view presented in this book shows a mix of beliefs that seem to be pulling from commonly shared ideas about regions in America and the people who live in them, the other views of the American dialect landscape presented reveal the importance of place, local categories, and proximity in descriptions of local linguistic (and sociocultural) phenomena.

Chapter 4 begins to tell the story of the South as a much-maligned locale, even for Southerners themselves. Building on the ideas set forth in Chapter 3 about the national picture, a zoomed-in version of the map leads us to an understanding of Southernness as inescapably connected to rather negative ideologies. The picture of planets employed in this data analysis is one of self-fulfilling patterns and of habit. Those national understandings of the South as home to hicks, hillbillies, and rednecks finds its way into the beliefs of Southerners describing their own dialect landscapes, even using these labels (usually derogatorily) to describe their home locales. Chapter 5, in exploring the more local understandings of these labels, provides for a view that is perhaps less negative – that is, using place as an overarching conceptualization of geographic space, culture, and practice allows us to recognize the role of experience, and not just stereotype, in understanding these individual positionings for the region. Yet, especially for Kentucky respondents, whose location is at the northernmost border of the South in numerous depictions of the region (see Cramer and Montgomery 2016), those negative beliefs loom large, and they construct within their own state a South/non-South dichotomy with eastern Kentucky and the rest of the state that uses fractal recursivity (Irvine & Gal 2000) to fully situate the negativity of Southernness in the Appalachian portion of the state.

In this process of othering, Kentuckians have made explicit the notion that they accept the broader stereotypes of Southernness as an appropriate designation for eastern Kentucky, relegating those dialects to the bottom of the dialect hierarchy within the state. One of the authors is a faculty member at a university in Kentucky, and her own experience with students from various portions of the state is that this is exactly how it plays out in real life. Students from eastern Kentucky often complain that their Louisville and Lexington counterparts especially like to poke fun at their accents. Then, upon returning to

Appalachia for the holidays, they are met with distain from family members who believe their relative has gotten 'above their raising' while away at college. They must learn to walk the linguistic tightrope, switching appropriately lest they be mocked. This experience is not likely particular to college students, and the fact that the map drawers made this same distinction suggests that it is a well-understood phenomenon for many Kentuckians.

No Southerner or speaker of a stigmatized variety will be surprised to read this previous paragraph. It is well-known (e.g. Lippi-Green 2012) that stigmatized varieties are often subjected to discrimination. What may be surprising, however, is that the fractal relationship exists and helps maintain both the larger-level 'North vs. South' ideology and the internal 'us vs. them' dynamics of a specific place in the South. The need to physically separate one's own speech from a nearby stigmatized variety has been seen in numerous perceptual dialectology studies. Indeed, in Preston (1989), southern Indiana respondents produced views of Kentucky that are quite negative, conforming to the pattern showing that all Kentuckians are likely held in the lower position in almost all other depictions of the South. Connecting this further to a belief structure that takes both national-level stereotypes and local-level experiences into consideration allows us to reconcile these facts that might otherwise seem counterintuitive.

But it's not all bad. Chapter 5 reveals that the 'good vs. bad' dichotomy is not the only salient level of distinction at the local level. Indeed, while 'Southern vs. Northern' and 'urban vs. rural' still maintain a strong hold on the perceptions of the most proximate locations, more labels and descriptions emerge with enhanced details that showcase the importance of solidarity and connectedness. It is a necessary reconciliation that Southerners must grapple with; their home is their home, and it is often important for them to maintain a sense of pride in their truly local places. Yet this positive view exists within the same belief planet in which they acknowledge those regional- and national-level stereotypes that guide their own larger views of the dialect landscape. These individual understandings of place give us a glimpse of this type of reconciliation, indicating that geographic proximity is a strong force against negative perceptions and that the on-the-ground categorizations that real speakers use to describe linguistic variation serve an important function in recognizing the role of place in linguistic perceptions.

Planets and perceptions

So, are the planets mostly made out of negative or positive ideas? According to our data, the answer is both. We know some words, like *hillbilly*, have been reclaimed (e.g. Chen 1998) and, in some cases are used to positively align with whatever a hillbilly identity might entail. We also know that some descriptions rely on media-based stereotypes designed to present a certain group in a specific (often negative) light. For example, references to 'Southern belles' are almost necessarily references to media presentations of Southerners as espousing certain beliefs related to gentility and civility, and as people who participate in a particular kind of Southern culture tied up with those beliefs. Either way, our understanding of the planets of belief metaphor is that people draw on experiences, stereotypes, and habits in understanding the stimuli we encounter. It does not matter if our beliefs align with reality. These systems we carry, created unconsciously, are what we use to understand our worlds. Therefore, it is of little importance whether we, as researchers, think it is good or bad that people rely on stereotypes in these tasks. It simply is. Those stereotypes, whether positive, negative, or neutral, are part of how people describe the geographical locations we have asked them to describe.

What may be of theoretical or methodological import is that the perceptions portrayed in these tasks are often very simplistic, caricature-like descriptions of whole regions, people, and speech patterns. It seems, then, that no matter how neutral the descriptions are, the fact that participants do not provide much at all in terms of complexity, nuance, or richness makes them, in a sense, negative, or at least reduced. What these variations potentially show us is that the cognitive map that participants have and portray in these tasks can look very different depending on the scale of the map. National-level maps showed more unmarked territories than maps at other scales. Participants tended to provide meaningful labels for the regions they drew and rarely provided additional commentary about the regions left unmarked. There were no comments like 'I don't know', 'I don't care', or 'nobody lives here', indicating a lack of concern about their presentation of those regions as blank. On the other hand, countless maps of a single state involved fully categorizing every geographic corner that was presented, as if to indicate that all people have some kind of language variety that is worthy of description. And while, overall, we found a great deal of variation, structural similarities like this, where the scale of the map conditions the responses, are astonishingly consistent. It is hard to escape the proposition that there is a set of beliefs about language and its speakers that the respondents share. Those commonalities, as conditioned by the maps, either buy into stereotypes that are widely distributed throughout American culture or highlight the importance of those local categorizations that community members share. As future researchers consider the kinds of perceptual dialectological questions that are relevant to their quests for understanding language variation and change, it is important that these issues of scale and detail are considered.

Perhaps we can find broad trends that exist in the data, and those are where we can find new linguistic information. But this does not mean that the individual beliefs presented are not also valuable. As we saw in Chapter 5, it is likely that localized views not only provide more details about the place under consideration, they also reveal how individual respondents use variations in descriptions of the dialect landscape to align with some groups and places and disalign with others. It may be that, at the local level, these kinds of perceptions say more about an individual's identity affiliations than they do about the actual dialect landscape they are trying to portray. To understand this idea, we need to understand how language and identity plays a role in perception.

The role of language and identity in perception

Linguistic studies of identity tend to focus on specific, socially constructed categories like gender or nationality. There are many different approaches available for the analysis of identity in linguistic research. For example, Le Page and Tabouret-Keller's (1985) linguistic theory of ACTS OF IDENTITY attempts to capture the generalizations of identity construction and the ways in which linguistic performance aids in this construction. When we conceive of these identities within a sociocultural paradigm, they are seen as dynamic, not static, emerging within the context of an interaction 'through the combined effects of structure and agency' (Bucholtz 1999:209). The interactional component is key; Bucholtz and Hall (2005) describe identity as 'the social positioning of the self and other' (2005:586). Thus, identity is not only about an individual. It is about the ways in which we describe others, which can often say more about the individual describing than it does about the one being described (e.g. Galasiński & Meinhof 2002). This focus on the dialogic relationship of the self and other makes identity construction an obvious additional task completed during the collection of perceptual dialectology data, especially in the form of mental maps.

When individuals draw a region, they indicate that the people enclosed in that region belong to a particular group, with a particular label and particular practices associated with them. In doing so, they either choose to enclose their own home region in that same region, thus choosing to align with that group, or they enclose their home region elsewhere, indicating that they belong to some other group. In many research paradigms, the task of determining what separates 'us' from 'them' can be difficult. Yet, this is exactly what the perceptual dialectology paradigm sets out to discover. In drawing their mental maps, providing labels, and describing dialect areas, participants draw on many kinds of information, including stereotypes, attitudes, and ideologies. In describing themselves and others, they use their belief planets to guide their presentations of identities.

The fact that this research paradigm almost necessitates the use of 'us vs. them' dichotomies, a fact that was revealed repeatedly in the data presented in earlier chapters, suggests that it is, in and of itself, a task that sets out to understand how in-groups develop. The beauty of the methodology is that it removes some of the outsider nature of the researcher and relies on the participants to explicitly show where the divisions are. In discussing the difficulties some researchers find in determining the relevant identity groups, Bucholtz and Hall suggest that

> [i]t is not easy for an outside observer to determine when a group of people should be classified as 'alike,' nor is it obvious on what grounds such a classification should be made, given the infinitude ways in which individuals may vary from one another. Hence, externally imposed identity categories

generally have at least as much to do with the observer's own identity position and power stakes as with any sort of objectively describable social reality.

(2004:370)

A connection between the kind of perceptual dialectology used in this book and the frameworks for understanding identity construction set forth by Bucholtz and Hall (2004, 2005) is quite obvious. Their framework, which is based on the semiotic nature of the processes of identification, indicates four such processes: practice, indexicality, ideology, and performance. For these authors, identity is 'an outcome of cultural semiotics that is accomplished through the production of contextually relevant sociopolitical relations of similarity and difference, authenticity and inauthenticity, and legitimacy and illegitimacy' (2004:382). The focus, then, is not only on how identities are formed but also why. We can take this framework as a basis for understanding the identity processes at work in mental map creation, which we have argued is itself formed in relation to the planets of belief held by the map drawer.

Practice refers to 'habitual social activity, the series of actions that make up our daily lives' (Bucholtz & Hall 2004:377). It draws on Bourdieu's (1977) notion of 'habitus', in which aspects of culture and belief systems are seen as durable and acquired through the repetition of life experiences. For Bourdieu, language is one such practice. We can see how those habits are the foundation of our planets of belief forming. Therefore, it is crucial to elicit and recognize this context, and as we have shown in the previous chapters, the tools of perceptual dialectology allow for that.

Indexicality is 'the semiotic operation of juxtaposition, whereby one entity or event points to another' (Bucholtz & Hall 2004:378). As with practice, repetition is important; if we see smoke, and discern that it was caused by fire, a pattern that certainly repeats itself over time, then we will necessarily see smoke as an index of fire. In language, this means that certain linguistic forms, over time, become intrinsically linked to certain kinds of speakers, eventually taking the form of social stereotypes. This pattern of behavior was clearly depicted in the makeup of the planets of belief on every level: national, regional, and local.

As discussed in Chapter 1, ideology is about the cultural belief systems of individuals, which means that linguistic ideologies are the beliefs associated with language. In their description of indexicality, we see links between linguistic forms and types of speakers. As such, the beliefs about language can turn into beliefs about speakers (Bucholtz & Hall 2004). It is exactly these kinds of ideology that are elicited in perceptual dialectology projects like the ones discussed in this book.

Finally, the process of performance is the deliberate social display of identities. As with any performance, the audience, those present for the performance, play a vital role in evaluating and constructing the performer's production of identity. This need not be in reference to actual stage performances; linguistic anthropologists describe linguistic performance in daily life, in which certain ideologies are brought to light in the (often exaggerated) performance of an identity. We have shown in our data that parts of those identities can be captured in perceptual dialectology research and allow the planets of belief to emerge from the identity performance.

How can this idea of planets be useful to non-experts?

Some people long for comfort in interactions. Others relish in the conflict interactions can create. Either way, interactions involve change. People are changed by their numerous and varied exchanges with others. Yet, we say that change is hard, that people are the way they are, and that we cannot hope to change people through action (or inaction). Recall our example of the *y'all*-using college professor. For those who indexically link Southern speech features with ignorance AND have fairly strong belief planets encompassing this notion, a simple interaction with this professor is unlikely to change them. The discordance between using *y'all* and being educated is too far of a leap. As we said, the person is faced with the option of completely changing their belief system because of this one interaction or writing it off as an anomaly. It appears, at least based on the research we have explored in this book, that most people choose the latter.

But we also know it because of the ways in which stereotypes persist. Hollywood continues to make billions off the uneducated hillbilly trope. Politicians become embroiled in controversy because of off-handed remarks, tweets, and various other forms of communication that maintain the linguistic status quo. Content creators in countless media outlets use shorthand images and misconstrued discourse to portray linguistic minorities and other non-standard speakers in a negative light. In this sense, the stereotypes not only loom large in the minds of people who have little experience with the groups being stereotyped; the stereotypes BECOME the reality, especially for those people who have not had the interactions that could change them. The stereotype is truth, and those minimal interactions fall short of being strong enough to make these kinds of changes.

Furthermore, as we have discussed, these kinds of disruptions to our belief structures are quite difficult. As humans, we are categorizers. We prefer to categorize in the most efficient way possible. The most efficient way to categorize the *y'all*-ing professor is to deny the possibility. We assume this speaker is the exception, not the rule. We do not wish to make changes to our ways of thinking. The planet, firmly situated in its orbit, stays put, and our beliefs about this exception are clouded by the larger stereotypes that dominate our thinking of people who sound this way.

What if it is not the exception? What if, in our day-to-day dealings with Southerners, over time, we come to realize the stereotype for what it is – an oversimplification, exaggeration, or simple falsehood? Perhaps, over time, our planets can change in this gradual way. Someone who had never met a Southerner may very well lean on the stereotypes until moving to the South. Then it becomes more difficult for the belief planet to stay intact. When the only input to perceptions are media depictions and overzealous grammar police, the picture of speakers of non-standard varieties is likely to be very ugly. Yet, it seems possible that experience with speakers and an understanding of the nature of language can do a lot to positively impact these perceptions. Anecdotally, the authors of this book have taught for numerous years at Southern universities, and they find that students who are exposed to the ideas that 1) all languages change, 2) all languages exhibit internal variation, 3) all speech varieties and languages are linguistically equal (but may differ in social prestige), and 4) dialectal variation is indicative of differences (in upbringing, in exposure, etc.), not of deficits, show increased awareness and acceptance of various ways of speaking.

Our argument in this book, then, is that knowledge is power. A person has the power to change their beliefs about language simply by becoming more knowledgeable about both their own preconceived notions and about how language actually works. While we do not wish to overestimate the objectivity of people, as Carroll (2016:111–12) cautions, we have learned, through our research (and teaching in the South), that people need more information than they are getting with respect to language. People use these linguistic stereotypes in their real worlds, with real people, to varying degrees of success. This is what perceptual dialectology is all about:

> It seems a reasonable assumption that perceptions of language and language use in [a society with an institutional standard] would have influence on the shape of the language itself, that is, be important factors in change. Even if such popular views of language, particularly those of language variation, are not primarily contributors to rule-making and modification, they are not a bit the less interesting. As a part of a speech community's set of beliefs about language and use, they are essential knowledge for an approach to linguistics which emphasizes societal and interactional context.
>
> (Preston 1989:2–3)

It is possible that we are preaching to the choir in some sense. If someone picks up this book, perhaps they are already in agreement with us. If the book is used in a class, perhaps the people who have chosen to enroll are as well. What we hope to have conveyed over the course of the book is a sense that linguists and students of linguistics play a role in shaping how people view language. We think critically about how language operates, and we have a wealth of knowledge that many people may never encounter in a formalized educational setting. And not all linguists value the opinions of nonlinguists in their own research and teaching programs. Lastly, those who adhere to the idea of a standard variety need to recognize when and how their perceptions about language use are not based in the structural realities of language as a complex system.

Making language seem at the same time more and less complex for people is a difficult task. Our focus on beliefs has emphasized how established the beliefs people hold can be, especially when those beliefs benefit the person who holds them. For the normative, middle-class, upwardly mobile white person in the United States, the assumption that everyone has access to and the desire to acquire Standard English is a belief that benefits them. Additionally, those who do not use it, rather, choose to not use the Standard in favor of some other variety are seen as somehow lacking in their personhood also benefits their status and supports their own linguistic choices. This dichotomy, however, is much too simplistic for the reality of language structure and use. Learning what these beliefs are and how strongly they are held, as we have tried to show here, is the first step toward being able to help people understand the more nuanced views of language that are discussed within linguistics as a discipline.

References

Bourdieu, Pierre. 1977. *Outline of a theory of practice*. Cambridge: Cambridge University Press.

Bucholtz, Mary. 1999. "Why be normal?": Language and identity practices in a community of nerd girls. *Language in Society* 28.203–23.

Bucholtz, Mary, and Kira Hall. 2004. Language and identity. *A companion to linguistic anthropology*, ed. by A. Duranti, 369–94. Malden, MA: Blackwell.

Bucholtz, Mary, and Kira Hall. 2005. Identity and interaction: A sociocultural linguistic approach. *Discourse Studies* 7.4–5.585–614.

Carroll, Sean. 2016. *The big picture: On the origins of life, meaning, and the universe itself*. New York: Penguin.

Chen, Melinda Yuen-Ching. 1998. "I am an animal!": Lexical reappropriation, performativity, and queer. *Engendering Communication: Proceedings from the Fifth Berkeley Women and Language Conference*, 128–40. Berkeley, CA.

Cramer, Jennifer, and Chris Montgomery (eds.) 2016. *Cityscapes and perceptual dialectology: Global perspectives on non-linguists' knowledge of the dialect landscape*. Berlin: Mouton de Gruyter.

Galasiński, Dariusz, and Ulrike H. Meinhof. 2002. Looking across the river: German-Polish border communities and the construction of the other. *Journal of Language and Politics* 1.1.23–58.

Irvine, Judith, and Gal Susan. 2000. Language ideology and linguistic differentiation. *Regimes of language: ideologies, polities, and identities*, ed. by Paul Kroskrity, 35–83. Santa Fe, NM: School of American Research Press.

Le Page, R.B., and Andrée Tabouret-Keller. 1985. *Acts of identity: Creole-based approaches to language and ethnicity*. Cambridge, UK: Cambridge University Press.

Lippi-Green, Rosina. 2012. *English with an accent*. 2nd edition. New York: Routledge.

Preston, Dennis R. 1989. *Perceptual dialectology: Nonlinguists' views of areal linguistics*. Dordrecht, the Netherlands: Foris.

AUTHOR INDEX

SUBJECT INDEX